God's Love Letters

God's Love Letters

Shawn Kilgarlin

iUniverse, Inc.
New York   Bloomington

God's Love Letters

Note: Unless otherwise noted, the Biblical passages quoted come from the
Application Study Bible, New Living Translation. Other translations used
include: *King James Version (KJV), New King James Version (NKJV), New
International Version (NIV)*, and *The Living Bible (TLB)*.

iUniverse books may be ordered through booksellers or by contacting:

iUniverse
1663 Liberty Drive
Bloomington, IN 47403
www.iuniverse.com
1-800-Authors (1-800-288-4677)

ISBN: 978-1-4401-5639-7 (sc)
ISBN: 978-1-4401-5638-0 (dj)
ISBN: 978-1-4401-5640-3 (ebook)

Printed in the United States of America

iUniverse rev. date: 11/09/2009

Contents

Foreword vii

Chapter 1: Filling My Soul with Godly Love 1

Chapter 2: Recognizing the Power of God's Love 5

Chapter 3: The Characteristics of God's Love for Us. . . . 9

☐ The Characteristics of Love 11

☐ Love Is Patient. 14

☐ Love: For Better or For Worse 16

☐ Love Is Not Revengeful 17

☐ Love Your Enemies 19

☐ Love Is Kind. 20

☐ Love Endures 23

☐ Love Is Compassionate 25

☐ Love Is Passionate 27

Chapter 4: God's Love for Us Endures All Things 29

Chapter 5: Let Christ Show You How to Worship Him . 37

☐ God's Love Brings Peace 39

☐ The Power of Humility 40

☐ Ten Ways to Keep Your "Humble Meter" in Balance .42

☐ Enjoy Your Childlike Faith 44

☐ Prayer 45

☐ Ask God to Open the Door to His House 45

☐ Prayer 49

☐ Fifteen Ways to Praise the Lord 50

☐ Instructions for Worship 52

☐ Five Good Reasons to Worship. 53

☐ Judging Others .53

☐ Declare War Against the Devil! 55

☐ Christ Is the Only Fair Judge! 55

☐ Forgive One Another 57

☐ The Scriptures Tell Us How to Produce Good Fruit . .58

☐ The Balance of Giving and Receiving 59

☐ Give Compassion 62

☐ Prayer 63

Chapter 6: Choosing God's Will for Your Life. 65
- ☐ Prayer 69
Chapter 7: What is God's Plan? 73
- ☐ Prayer 74
- ☐ Free Yourself. 79
- ☐ How to Recognize God's Plan for Your Life 81
- ☐ Twenty-Five Names for Our God! 83
- ☐ Prayer 84
- ☐ Releasing Anger and Resentment. 85
- ☐ Pray Every Day for Forgiveness 91
- ☐ When to Forgive 92
- ☐ Prayer 93
Chapter 8: God's Gift of Patience 95
- ☐ Trials and Suffering 99
- ☐ My Message to All of You. 100
- ☐ Prayer 101
Chapter 9: Building a Relationship with Christ 103
- ☐ Reading the Bible 104
- ☐ Prayer and Meditation 106
- ☐ Prayer 111
- ☐ Ten Ways to Live a Redeemed Life 113
- ☐ How to Apply Solidarity to Your Life 118
- ☐ How to Consecrate and Dedicate Yourself to the Lord 118
- ☐ Prayer 119
- ☐ Dealing with Affliction and Adversity 120
- ☐ Give Your Soul to God 121
- ☐ Handle Illness and Sorrow with God's Love 123

Foreword

I'm from Louisiana, and I love to eat. I'm passionate about food, and I'm passionate about buying and preparing my food. In addition, I'm passionate about my work, and I love what I do. I'm also passionate about being a good wife and mother. In fact, I'm passionate about helping others, and that's why I wrote this book especially for you!

I love letters—passionately! I'm not much for writing letters, but I sure do love to receive them—and read them, sometimes over and over!

The New Testament is a book made up of a veritable bouquet of love letters. These are love letters about the story of God. These inspirational letters talk about the love of God, and they are the truth. They teach us how to know and love Him intimately. They are letters to *you* from God. **(John 17:17)** Seeking and reading the Word of God strengthened my relationship with Him.

During nearly all my times of adversity in life, I've looked to the Bible for guidance and sought spiritual comfort there, and I've always found it.

When I was very young, my uncle advised me to read—and read I did. The Bible was always a source of stories, real-life stories! I remember thinking, "What better book in the world could there be?" And years later, I *still* think this way, and believe it so wholeheartedly that I would not have lived my life to the fullest until I shared this with you.

Like most people, I've faced times of adversity; my life certainly wasn't always rosy. I've looked into the dark well of what I perceived to be "nothingness" many times, and one time in particular, I nearly fell in. Therefore, I have no doubt in my mind that the grace of our Lord Jesus Christ truly and absolutely saved me.

Chapter 1:
Filling My Soul with Godly Love

Today, I own a successful health-care business. My life is happy and in order now, but it started out rather badly. In short, I put God and my love for Christ in the "backseat" of my life. I ended up letting my seemingly all-important lifestyle and career drive the car. At least that's what I did until that car ran off the road.

When I was just out of college and only twenty-five, I felt quite enterprising. I'd done well in school and put myself through it by working hard (more about that later). By the time I graduated, I was ready to put that degree to work.

I went out on my own and started a small business from scratch. Before the first year was over, it had grown substantially. I had twenty-five employees, and I was working eighty hours a week.

Also during this time in my life, I'd met the love of my life and was about to get married. Everything seemed to have fallen right into place, although I admit I was a little overwhelmed by all the activity. But I thought I deserved my success! It had been a hard, long road getting there, and I wanted my day in the sun.

I thought I was sailing along, but then, boom! I encountered extreme troubles in my business, which left me feeling like a fragile glass ball I'd been holding had shattered into a thousand little shards that left cuts and open wounds everywhere in my life, both professional and personal. The details aren't important here, but this was a time of extreme suffering for my family and me.

That was my first real "wake-up call" about conducting business *and* leading a spiritual life. I finally understood that it meant more than attending church regularly. Living a spiritual life meant being true and consistent at home and especially in business. The devil will find you most vulnerable in business, especially when you're young, reeling with success and money, and heading an organization on your own.

That early experience taught me a lot about business, but the more important lesson I learned was about how God and His loving Son truly *want* to work with us, day in and day out, even in the midst of an eighty-hour week!

After this trouble settled down, my husband and I sold our home and moved to Shreveport to live with his mom, which turned out to be one of the best things we ever did. I got back on my feet and landed a great PR job for a top hotel chain, and we started over. My husband was able to recoup the interest from my business and keep it going on his own. In this second phase, we went from twenty-five employees to only four, and then from barely making ends meet to making very good profits.

We are still in love, we are both successful, and I'm in the best shape of my life. My husband was faithful to me and to our life together through those rough times, but I strongly believe that our faith in God was the one thing that really got us through.

Chapter 2:
Recognizing the Power of God's Love

I remember being so depressed and anxious before we moved back to Shreveport. I was literally shaking on the inside—a nervous wreck. Soon though, I found my own remedy: whenever this happened, I just picked up the Bible and started reading Psalms. I read and read, just like I had when I was a child, until I was calm again.

I was amazed. I felt something, and I realized something was different. This calmness was better than any prescription drug, tranquilizer, or antidepressant, and it intrigued me. When I accepted Christ into my life again, my spiritual growth began.

I love God so much now because I remember what my life was like without Him. I was lost, confused, angry, anxious, and sad. I felt this way because I didn't have an intimate, personal relationship with Christ. Sure, I went to church every Sunday. However, having only church and prayer had left me raw and hungry inside.

So, I began a road to discovery. I studied the Word of God, I prayed, and I surrendered myself wholly to Him. Then I put myself on a path: I strove to become Christ-like.

This was a very gradual process, but also extremely fulfilling. My circumstances started changing miraculously. I was determined and cheerful. Oh boy, was I full of enthusiasm! I found a true sense of peace in the tranquility of soul, including peace of mind in all conditions and under all circumstances. My feelings of despair, anger, resentment, pride, irritability, and fear all left. My emotions no longer swayed my faith, and all my imperfections seemed to disappear. Christ consoled me. His spirit dwelled in me. I felt alive again, full of joy even in the worst conditions.

Everyone thought I was crazy. Maybe I was—I was crazy for the love of God! It's funny how people will look askance at you when you're happy, when you're ecstatic about life. I was living on a natural high, but no one around me could really understand how or why. They just didn't "get it."

"How do you stay so happy all the time?" people asked. "How do you get excited about the smallest things? What is your secret anyway?"

It was then that I realized I had a message to share. I'm here to show you that when you truly find Christ, how beautifully, miraculously, and almost effortlessly it will change your life.

Love is the greatest, most gratifying feeling in the

world. We all have an inner desire to be loved that comes from deep within our souls. To love and to be loved is our reason for being.

It is not good for man to be alone. I will make a companion who will help him. (**Genesis 2:18**)

In the English language, there is only one word for love, but in the Greek language, there are many different types of love, and when we understand them, we better understand how to love different people in many different ways.

Chapter 3:
The Characteristics of God's Love for Us

There are four different types of love, which are expressed and derived from the Greek language:

☐ *Eros*—This is a love between the sexes, that is, sexual love between a man and woman.

☐ *Philia*—This is the love we have for friends and those we encounter along the way during our lives.

☐ *Storge*—This is a family love, the love between a child and his mother or father and vice versa.

☐ *Agape*—This is Godly, Christian love, the love we should all strive for. It's all about desiring, hoping for, and sincerely wanting others to enjoy goodwill.

Although the Greeks have a few different names for

love, there is only one true love: Godly love … *agape* love. Godly love is the most powerful force on Earth.

Love is defined in the *NLT Dictionary/Concordia* as the ultimate expression of God's loyalty, purity, and mercy extended toward His people—to be reflected in human relationships of brotherly concern, marital fidelity, and adoration for God.

How much do you *love* the person you *like the least*? Think about this for a moment. I'm not talking about someone you "hate"; we'll get to that later. But just think for a moment, as your answer to that question shows how much you love God. It makes you think, doesn't it? You should love *everyone* with Godly love, as anything less won't do.

You may think it's impossible to show Godly love to everyone. Well, with God in control of your soul, the impossible becomes possible. And remember: we're only human. Some people will act rudely no matter what you do or what you say, and what you tell yourself is that's just how they are, rude and unreachable. But these are the people we need to love the most.

I'm not saying you should initiate a close, intimate relationship with them, but I am telling you, you must show them *agape* love, Godly love. You must forgive them if you believe they have betrayed you or hurt your feelings on purpose. This is where your job as a Christian comes in—to love your enemies as you love yourself.

Despite what you may think, it's *not* impossible! Instead of being rude in return, which is vengeful, or allowing or accepting the rudeness coming from these people, start being kindhearted and warm. Start saying pleasant things about that person to that person.

This works even when the other person's behavior goes beyond rude. For example, if you are a parent, and your child comes home and tells you that your ex-spouse or another relative has been saying derogatory things about you, just calmly tell your child not to worry. Then, you can ask your child to pray for this relative. Say positive things about the other person while praying with your child.

Sometimes all it takes is sending a thoughtful greeting card to someone whom you believe is your "enemy." This simple extension of love can lead to a peaceful resolution. If necessary, apologize for any of your past comments or actions that may have been hurtful, then ask if you can look for common ground.

It's sometimes a trying process. It may take years for that person to change. But in the meantime, don't waste your time worrying about it. Change yourself first. Open your mind! Learn to pray and love everyone with Godly love!

I promise that when given freely, your Godly love will flow out of you and rub off on your enemies. All you have to do is pray for them. God will begin to work in their lives and change them from the inside out. It's through this *agape* love, given freely, that the soul can be filled with joy.

The Characteristics of Love

Corinthians 13:4–7 lists fifteen characteristics of love:

> *Love is patient.*
> *Love is kind.*
> *Love is not jealous.*
> *Love is not boastful.*
> *Love is not proud.*

Love is not rude.
Love does not demand its own way.
Love is not irritable.
Love keeps no record of when it has been wronged.
Love is never glad about injustice.
Love rejoices whenever truth wins.
Love never gives up.
Love never loses faith.
Love is always hopeful.
Love endures through every circumstance.

This heavenly love comes directly from God. It is a gift from God and can only be obtained by the Holy Spirit.

And this expectation will not disappoint us. For we know how dearly God loves us, because he has given us the Holy Spirit to fill our hearts with his love. (**Romans 5:5**)

Agape love is divine love. We can only receive this gift of love if we love God and His Son, Jesus Christ. So, get into a real relationship with God's love. Don't just sit on the sidelines. Get involved!

Isaiah 54 states that chastisement is peace. Your peace is always available from the love of God, regardless of circumstances.

We should worship God today—right now—because we are redeemed. We were bought with a price: Jesus's blood.

I know I have found this divine love. I know Christ changed my whole life through his love. I can't help what happens to my brothers, my children, or my parents. All I know for certain is that Christ's love changed me—and it can change you, too.

When you have this divine love, it won't matter what anyone says about you. Because I am so infused with God's love, it truly doesn't bother me when people talk badly about me. I have God's love, and that's all that matters. We should love God, and give Him our ultimate admiration.

God's love is the most absolute love we can ever know. God has created a special family for us: He can be our mother, father, friend, comforter, provider, and deliverer. He sends His heavenly angels to camp around us. Isn't that wonderful? We have a host of angels waiting at our command. Guardian angels aren't just for children. They are sent as a token of God's love, and they remain with us until our time here on Earth is completed.

Name your angel—I've named mine. Speak to your angel every day with love, and learn to love unconditionally.

Place me like a seal over your heart, or like a seal on your arm. For love is as strong as death, and its jealousy is as enduring as the grave. Love flashes like fire, the brightest kind of flame. Many waters cannot quench love; neither can rivers drown it. If a man tried to buy love with everything he owned, his offer would be utterly despised. (**Song of Songs 8:6–7**)

If I could speak in any language in Heaven or on Earth, but didn't love others, I would only be making meaningless noises like a loud gong or a clanging cymbal. If I had the gift of prophecy, and knew all the mysteries of the future, and knew everything about everyone, but didn't love others, what good would I be? And even if I had the gift of faith so that I could speak to a mountain and make it move, without love I would be no good to anybody. If I gave everything I have to the poor, and even sacrificed my body, I could boast about it, but if I didn't love others, I would be of no value whatsoever.

Love is patient and kind. Love is not jealous or boastful, proud or rude. Love does not demand its own way. Love is not irritable, and it keeps no record of when it has been wronged. Love is never glad about injustice, but rejoices whenever the truth wins out. Love never gives up, never loses faith, is always hopeful, and endures through every circumstance.

Love will last forever, but prophecy and speaking in unknown languages and special knowledge will all disappear. Now we know only a little, and even the gift of prophecy reveals little! But when the end comes, these special gifts will all disappear. (**I Corinthians 13:1–10**)

Love Is Patient

I will confess this freely: I used to be a real slob!

Disorganization was one of my worst qualities—a very bad habit, to say the least. When I was first married, my husband and I got into arguments about my messiness. I'd get very upset and call my mother, complaining about how my husband was fussing at me for being messy.

My husband expected me to keep our house looking spotless, which required a lot of effort on my part. On the other extreme, Ron is very neat. When he came home, he'd always find something to complain about! At least that was the way I viewed it.

One of our major disputes was over my closet. I had a separate walk-in closet, and whenever Ron looked inside and saw piles of things on the floor, he'd get frustrated and complain. He couldn't understand why I wouldn't hang up my clothes. This perturbed me because I couldn't comprehend why my closet mattered to him. He had his own closet! I told him to stay out of my closet, and sometimes I called him a neat freak and stormed out. And so at least in my mind, Ron was a perfectionist and I was a slob.

I remember getting so upset about his annoying me about that closet, I once considered moving out. I was in tears when I called my mother to tell her my husband was crazy. I said he had no business going into my closet.

"Shawn, let me tell you a little secret about how I kept my marriage strong for so many years," my mother said.

I stubbornly dried my tears and listened.

"Sometimes you have to make things go their way. You have to give in and stop being selfish." She paused. "Shawn, do you love him?"

"Yes."

"Have you ever considered just hanging your pants up? Try it today. Hang your pants up. Show him what you've done. Give in a little bit, and be patient with him. He will come around."

I didn't like her advice, but I went ahead and hung *all* the clothes up in my closet. When Ron came home from work, I rushed to the door and told him I had a surprise for him. I showed him my closet, and he was so pleased. He took me out to dinner and was just ecstatic. I liked the praise and attention, so I made it a habit to keep my closet neat: a small compromise on my part, and one that made me feel better about myself. Over the years, Ron and I have learned to be patient with each other, and we've both evolved as individuals.

Love means being patient with each other's shortcomings. It means giving. It means going the extra step to make the other person happy. Sometimes that means changing yourself.

So, the next time you have a dispute with someone, ask yourself how you can be more patient. What can you do to resolve the problem?

Sometimes we need to submit to the situation, and things will always just work themselves out. For example, several years ago, I started collecting decorative boxes. I started using these boxes to stay organized, which turned into an actual hobby. I turned my negative quality into a positive one.

I now have hundreds of boxes. Everything in my house has a place. I get excited every time I get a new box, and I always find something to organize. My house is now organized, and it makes us both content. I am no longer a slob, and Ron is no longer such a perfectionist. We met in the middle. We adjusted by having patience with each other through love.

Be humble and gentle. Be patient with each other, making allowance for each other's faults because of your love. **(Ephesians 4:2)**

Love: For Better or For Worse

In any loving relationship, there will be times where one person just doesn't feel intimate. It may not be your fault; in fact, it's usually no one's fault.

When I was pregnant, Ron and I didn't have much sex. I started to worry and feel rejected, so I went out and bought about six "relationship" books. Every book said the same thing: "Sex is important for a healthy relationship. If there is no sex, leave the relationship; it's unhealthy." Though I read this over and over, I just didn't believe it. If I'd taken this advice, I would have viewed my relationship as unhealthy—and divorced my husband!

I knew my husband loved me, and I knew we had a healthy relationship. Yet I couldn't understand why he didn't want to make love to me while I was pregnant. However, I did know he wasn't cheating on me.

We were married in the eyes of God. So, I felt happiness without sex. I never pressured him or demanded to know why; I was just patient with him. I did end up paying attention to one very important "relationship" book: the Bible. It told me to stay with my husband for better or for worse.

Sometimes we have to just wait a problem out. We may give love and not receive it back right away. At other times, we need to wait for love in return. Love is grand! Love is also a mystery, and true love will always make your soul smile—even if you're not wearing a smile on your face every single day!

Ron and I have been married for nine years, and we're happier than ever. Life is grand and good. But marriage is sometimes both sweet and sour, and you have to be prepared to make it through the sour patches. But boy, is the sweet worth the wait!

Love Is Not Revengeful

Sometimes people do hateful and destructive things that cause us grief and sorrow. Love is the answer to these problems, not vengeance.

You have heard that the law of Moses says, "Love your neighbor and hate your enemy. But I say, love your enemies!" Pray for those who persecute you! In that way, you will be acting as true children of your Father in Heaven. For He gives His sunlight to both the evil and the good, and He sends rain on the just and on the unjust too. If you love only those who love you, what good is that? Even corrupt tax collectors do that much. If you are kind only to your friends, how are you different from anyone else? Even pagans do that. (**Matthew 5:43–47**)

Getting revenge means reacting in a hateful manner to something bad done to us—it means getting even. Our adversaries have made us so mad that we become filled with rage, and soon hate takes over. The next thing we know, we're plotting a way to avenge ourselves. If this sounds familiar, then you don't love as God commands us to love. You either don't truly know the Lord, or you are letting the devil take over.

So, don't retaliate when people say unkind things about you. Don't stoop to the level of the devil. Instead, pay them back with a blessing. That is what God wants you to do, and He will bless you for it. For the scriptures say: *If you want a happy life and good days, keep your tongue from speaking evil and keep your lips from telling lies. Turn away from evil and do good. Work hard at living in peace with others. The eyes of the Lord watch over those who do right, and His ears are open to prayers. But the Lord turns His face against those who do evil.* (**I Peter 3:9–12**)

Don't get caught up in vengeance. When you begin digging a ditch for your enemies, you are actually setting a trap for yourself. What comes around goes around, and you will eventually fall in the ditch yourself.

I truly believe this theory that what you do will come back at you, as I've have seen it happen time and time again. Instead of revenge, you must believe in the Lord, always strive to do the right thing, and stay on a clear path.

Love Your Enemies

Do you know why I love my enemies? Because they keep me on my toes. They are the biggest challenge to my Christianity. What a gift that is! Just consider it: when your enemies challenge you, and you respond to them with patience and love, it puts you on a higher spiritual level.

Every time I am patient through love, my soul is elevated to a higher place. Let the enemy have your old place. Climb up the ladder to a new level of supernatural ecstasy. Think of it this way: while your enemies are fighting you, you could be reaching new heights in your spirituality!

The only way to get to the Kingdom of Heaven is upward. So, it actually should be exciting when your enemies persecute you, because this shows God's love for you! Don't fight your enemies—let God fight them for you.

God knows and sees everything. God says, "I've seen what you have been going through. You have been persecuted and deceived. Just keep on going, and I will fight the battle for you."

When you are full of revenge and send evil back, you put yourself on the same level as your enemies. However, if you take evil and reward it with good, God will fight your battles for you. But some people think, "I'll just get even just this *one* time."

Come on, now—God isn't a fool. God knows when you are doing wrong. Don't hinder your blessings by seeking revenge. When God sends His blessings down, you need to be ready to receive them. You need to be in the right position and in the right relationship, not out seeking vengeance.

Pray for your enemies; pray for the softening of their heart. It takes time and patience, but it *works*.

Love Is Kind

It's an all-too-common problem: the number of people who suffer with clinical depression is on the rise. Have you ever been kind to someone who is depressed? Have you noticed the difference it makes? A kind word, a friendly smile, and a true sense of loving compassion go a long way.

God wants us to share our love with everyone and to be kind. Fill your soul with Godly love, and change someone's life today. God *wants* us to share our love with everyone; it's why we're all here—all in this together here on Earth. Why would a loving God put us here to fight each other? Instead, He means for us to love and protect each other!

Be kindly affectionate to one another with brotherly love, in honor giving preference to one another. **(Romans 12:10)**

It may often seem that taking the path of least resistance means being unkind or uncaring. Why is that? How hard can it be to conjure up a smile anyway? But sometimes it can be difficult, particularly when we're having a bad day ourselves. When we're caught up in our own worldly problems, we don't think about kind love.

When Ron and I lived in Baton Rouge, Louisiana, we frequently visited his parents in Shreveport. It was a long four-and-a-half-hour drive with a newborn. Every time we arrived, my father-in-law, Richard, greeted us in the driveway and showered us with kindness. "Shawn, wow!" he'd say. "Look at you. You look so good. I love your hair."

He also called me "Slim"—"Hey, Slim, looking good," he'd say. He said similar things to my husband. "Ron, staying trim." He paid attention to us as if we were the only people on the planet. His kind words lifted my spirits when I was down.

When was the last time you were truly nice to someone? I'm not talking about your everyday kindness, but the kindness that comes from Godly love, the kindness that requires supernatural strength to achieve. Richard made me feel so good about myself, I began to adopt that feeling about me as well. When I returned home, I started mimicking Richard's actions. It took a while, though. I had to pray for this kindly love, as it didn't come naturally.

I used it on my mom when she dyed her gray hair a lovely black. Instead of being the "old Ginger" and noticing but not saying much, I spoke up: "Mom, wow! Look at your hair. It makes you look ten years younger. It accents your eyes." And that was true! I wish you could have seen the twinkle in her eyes. She smiled like a little girl, and she was in a great mood the rest of the day.

So, try showing kindness—it works! Try it on your spouse. After years of being together, we may forget how to show kindness. But being kind can make a dormant relationship come alive. And simple compliments can change someone's mood in an instant.

Let me elaborate on the old saying: there's a fine line between love and hate. That means that we find ourselves doing hateful things to the ones we love. However, with Godly love, we can change that behavior before we leave permanent scars on others.

Crossing the love–hate line happens more often than we realize. We may be irritable and end up in a heated discussion with a loved one. One thing leads to another, and suddenly our lack of self-control results in our burning bridges. Even those we love can get our blood boiling. Then all we can think about is being right, having the last word, and upsetting the other person.

Stop! Discover Godly love today. Remember, this is the love that does everything to glorify God. It's the love that is humble and has no pride. It's the love that isn't irritable or rude, no matter what the circumstances. It's selfless love.

Stand up for what's moral and right. Transform your mind. Don't act as the world teaches you to act. Convert your soul to a soul of love.

Do not conform any longer to the pattern of this world, but be transformed by the renewing of your mind. These you will be able to test and approve what God's will is—His good, pleasing and perfect will. (**Romans 12:2**)

Our minds have to be reformed. Be passionate about your journey to change. Tell yourself, "I will be morally sound in my senses."

The next time you become irritable and full of pride, transform your mind and hold your tongue. Be humble and you won't fall into the trap the devil has set for you. Sometimes we must take drastic action to stay on the love side of that fine line. The devil tries to wreak havoc in our lives in so many ways; he uses us, then sits back and laughs as we fail. The devil doesn't play fair.

The devil can take a simple discussion and turn it into a major fight, just to win our souls, just to get us to cross the line to hate. It's easier to cross the line. It's harder to stay in control. So pray for self-control.

God wants us to be righteous, to take a stand. He wants us to only speak words of kindness and never cross the fine line between love and hate.

Love Endures

Love never gives up, never loses faith, is always hopeful, and endures through every circumstance.

Love needs commitment, and love means compromise. Love always makes sacrifices.

I know a woman named Jami who really wanted a dog. But she'd just married Todd, who had allergies. So Jami had to sacrifice her love for animals for her husband's health.

Although Jami and Todd had been married for six months, Jami hadn't met Todd's parents, who lived out of town. For their first Christmas together, they made the trip to her in-laws. Unbeknownst to her, Todd had telephoned his mother and asked that she buy Jami a poodle as a surprise. He knew poodles produced the least shedding, so his allergic reaction would be manageable.

When they arrived, Jami met her new mother-in-law—and her new poodle. That day, she became a vessel of a new kind of love. Her husband had sacrificed his health and compromised to make his wife happy. This is Godly love, the selfless act of giving.

"Then you will call upon me and come and pray to me, and I will listen to you. You will seek me and find me when you seek me with all your heart. I will be found by you," declares the Lord, "and will bring you back from captivity. I

will gather you from all the nations and places where I have banished you," declares the Lord, "and will bring you back to the place from which I carried you into exile." (**Jeremiah 29:12–14**)

In our time of trouble, Ron and I used God's divine love to make it through. In the span of just a few months, we went from having it all to losing everything, but we turned to God's Word for help.

Jesus replied, "If anyone loves me, he will obey my teaching. My Father will love him, and we will come to him and make our home with him. He who does not love me will not obey my teaching. These words you hear are not my own, they belong to the Father who sent me. All that I have spoken while still with you." (**John 14:23–25**)

When we began serving the Lord, we found new hope that helped us endure.

Therefore, my dear brothers, stand firm. Let nothing move you. Always give yourself fully to the Lord, because you know that your labor in the Lord is not in vain. (**I Corinthians 15:58**)

We devoted ourselves to God's will and put Him in our heart. Our desire was only to do His will. *Oh my God; Your law is written in my heart.* (**Psalm 40:8**)

We had to learn to love again, God's way. Our love endured the trial, and adversity strengthened our characters. We had everything and then lost everything just within a few months, but oh, how wonderful are the rewards and blessings God has for those who love Him! We endured, and we passed the test through God's love.

Love Is Compassionate

Have you ever noticed when small children are playing and one gets upset, the others will try to comfort him or her? This is called compassion. Children, like animals, have natural compassion,

My Jack Russell Terrier, Lily, had compassion for my son, Cody. Every time Cody cried, Lily ran to his door and cried. She stayed awake until I finished feeding him. In doing so, Lily demonstrated she had compassion.

Compassion is being moved by another's suffering. Compassion appeals to human emotions. We are all born with compassion.

Jesus had compassion for Mary Magdalene, who was thought to be an adulteress (although I understand now that this assumption may not be true. In any case, she became one of his great friends and supporters.)

[Mary Magdalene's accusers] *said to Jesus, "Teacher, this woman was caught in the act of adultery. In the law, Moses commanded us to stone such women. Now, what do you?"* They were using this question as a trap in order to have a basis for accusing him. *But Jesus stepped down and started to write with his finger. When they kept on questioning him, he straightened up and said to them, "If any one of you is without sin, let him be the first to throw a stone at her." Again he stooped down and wrote on the ground again.*

At this, those who heard began to go away one at a time, the older ones first, until only Jesus was left, with the woman still standing there. Jesus straightened up and asked her, "Woman where are they? Has no one condemned you?"

"No one sir," she said.

"Then neither do I condemn you. Go now and sin no more," Jesus declared. (**John 8:4–11**)

Jesus had compassion for Mary, so he forgave rather than condemning her. Jesus doesn't condemn us, either. He came to save us. We should be compassionate and forgiving, just as Jesus was.

Have you lost your compassion? When you see someone in need of help, do you stop to help, or do you just walk on by? Did you feel compassion on September 11, 2001, even if you weren't directly affected? Did you feel the pain of others?

Jesus showed us how to be compassionate. He helped the poor, the weak, and the handicapped. Jesus told us to love our enemies and pray for those who persecute us, and to not judge others.

We are all spirits living in bodies, yet it is through our souls that we connect with others and feel their pain. When our children get hurt, we feel pain, too—and that's compassion.

Start today. Have compassion for others. If you can help someone in a time of crisis, do so with a tender heart, not with thoughts about what you will get in return.

"Is tasteless food eaten without salt, or is there flavor in the white of the egg? I refuse to touch it. Such food makes me ill." (**Job 6:6–7**)

Job was suffering and complaining. He needed compassion and love. Do you know someone like Job? Then show that person compassion today. You can show compassion just by listening.

Love Is Passionate

I started this book by talking about passion, my passion for God. But we all long for a certain kind of affectionate and passionate love that includes hugging, kissing, and touching. We don't always get that type of love. For example, my father was never affectionate toward me. He rarely said "I love you" in words. My mother was the same way. However, I always felt their love deep within my heart.

I was fortunate to have good parents who raised me well, even though I always longed for more physical affection. As a young adult, it was hard for me to accept someone who could love me passionately.

My husband, on the other hand, is very passionate about his family. His affectionate mother is his best friend. Ron's entire family is connected, emotionally and mentally, by body and spirit. They are always there for support, their arms open to express their love.

When I discovered this passionate love, I started imitating it and using it to show my love for my family. Surprisingly, my mother immediately opened up to it!

Then I asked my dad why he just said good-bye and then hung up the telephone after I expressed my love. I explained that this hurt my feelings. Once I confronted my dad, he started expressing his feelings of love. Now, when I tell my father in person that I love him, he tells me he loves me, too. However, he always seems embarrassed or shy. I've learned since then that this reticence simply stems from his own childhood during which he wasn't given love freely and openly either.

Chapter 4:
God's Love for Us Endures All Things

Some of you may not be as fortunate as I was in that you didn't have the love of one or both parents while growing up. However, no matter what happened to us in the past, we must look forward rather than backwards in order to be good parents to our children and show Godly love and forgiveness.

It's true that some parents make serious and unloving mistakes. They abandon their children, or don't pay child support. They may abuse drugs and/or alcohol or suffer from an untreated, undiagnosed mental illness. These issues make it impossible for them to fully care for their children, much less set a good example.

But what do you do when, twenty years later, these parents seek love and forgiveness? Do you forget what they've done to you? (No, that never works.) Do you shut them out? Or do you draw upon God's strength and show them Godly love?

John the Baptist lived on a diet of grasshoppers and honey. This isn't what I would choose to eat, even though I live on diets, as many of us do in these days of abundance. But John the Baptist did this for survival. John was Jesus's cousin, and he came to prepare the way for the Lord. One of the main things he preached was the need to listen to God's message. He taught others how to remodel and successfully learn from that message.

We often feel resentment and conflict in families, which means the gift of love that God freely gives us becomes lost in the shuffle. We start setting our own laws, we forgive only who we want to forgive, and so forth.

But if we continue on this road, we simply won't have time to reform our lives. We will get into the elevator and say, "Oops! I'm on the wrong elevator. This one is going down to hell. I'm supposed to be going up." Now it's too late!

God wants us to reform our lives through love. It's a monumental task, and we sometimes don't listen to Him. Then He asks us: why? The answer is that we didn't look within ourselves. We look at ourselves in the mirror and don't like what we see. We see anger, dissatisfaction, and emptiness—all signs of a lack of love. We sometimes end up making bad choices. We can get stuck in a rut and need someone to pull us out.

This might not describe you, but what about your parents? Did they make mistakes? Were they in a rut while you were growing up? Are you going to send them a lifeboat—or let them sink? Are you going to take an eye for an eye? Do you hold the attitude that because they abandoned you, it's okay for you to abandon them?

When you are secure within the comfort of God's love, you will see and understand that God will never abandon you, and neither should you ever abandon anyone. Instead, you must forgive.

The Lord gives us a choice to follow Him. If we do so, we will take the elevator upward to Heaven. If we don't, we will take the elevator to hell. It's that easy, and the choice is yours: He's not going to come over to your house, twist your arm, and say, "Hey, now you must follow me!" No, He won't do that at all. He puts the ball in your court. If you want to be a follower of His love, then it's up to you to volley it back to Him.

God always wants the best for you, but it's up to you to reform your life and live in love. God doesn't want you to be condemned, to be lost, or, in human terms, to become just a statistic. God gave Jesus every one of us. Jesus died for us at Calvary, purchasing our souls with his blood. Now Jesus wants to return us to his father. He has a place waiting for us.

"In my Father's house are many rooms. If it were not so, I would have told you. I am going there to prepare a place for you, I will come back and take you to be with me that you also may be where I am. You know the way to the place where I am going." (**John 14:2–4**)

God's love endures. God's love is truth. Therefore, it naturally follows that we should be true to one another. Jesus wants us to be a part of His love. Learn to look in the mirror and smile, and then start using that love and that smile to improve the lives of others. A smile opens up your heart, but a frown tells people to back away. Smile today and every day—don't frown and turn people away. Change your life today.

Reform your life so you can walk in the light of Christ. Focus on the love of God. He will give you the strength to help you carry it to the end, because true love like this endures.

"Only acknowledge your inequity that you have transgressed against the Lord your God, and have scattered your charms to alien deities under every green tree, and you have not obeyed my voice," says the Lord. **(Jeremiah 3:13 NKJV)**

God's love is everlasting; nothing can separate us from God's love.

"For I am persuaded that neither death nor life, nor angels nor principalities nor powers, nor things present nor things to come, nor height nor depth, nor any other created thing, shall be able to separate us from the love of God which is in Christ Jesus our Lord." **(Romans 8:38–39)**

Unless you have an intimate relationship with God, it will be hard for you to grasp His power. You see, *God is love.* **(I John 4:16)** Whenever you accept Christ into your life, and into your heart, your soul, your mind, and your spirit, you become a child of God. After you become a child of God, His love manifests itself into your soul. Jesus will live in you, and therefore, you will be led by the spirit of God.

For as many as are led by the Spirit of God, these are sons of God. For you did not receive the spirit of bondage again to fear, but you received the spirit of adoption by whom we cry out, "Abba, Father." The Spirit Himself bears witness with our spirit that we are children of God. **(Romans 8:14–16)**

Whenever God's spirit dwells in us, we start to love as God loves. We become compassionate, forgiving, unselfish, patient, and kind. We treat others with loving kindness. We aren't rude to others. We love others as we love ourselves.

I knew of a fine man named Joe whose story exemplifies the way love is patient, kind, unselfish, and enduring to the end. Joe became an angel to a little girl, Janet, when he was sixty years old. With the testimony of that little girl, my friend in Christ, his story will live on as witness to the good works God can do when we really put our egos aside, and live for God.

> ***Janet's Story*** (used with her permission)
>
> *When I was thirteen, my parents separated and subsequently divorced. I stayed with my father for a while in our family home. But little by little, everything fell apart. Years earlier, my father had a drinking problem. The divorce pushed him over the edge, and he began drinking again. However, he was able to maintain his job as an insulator. He tried to raise me alone, but slowly his home life crumbled around him. The electricity, telephone, and water were all shut off because he didn't pay the bills. He had an ice chest in which he kept the bologna and bread we ate for days at a time. I still attended school, but I often spent the nights with a succession of friends so I could take a bath.*
>
> *One day, I became sick with asthma and called my mom's first husband, Joe, and ended up spending time with him. He taught*

me how to play checkers and dominoes, and he cooked me a steak for lunch every Saturday. When I was six or seven, he began taking me to LSU football games. Then he helped me take baton-twirling lessons so I could perform at halftime during my elementary school football games. Joe took me to visit the LSU twirlers and Golden Girls before the games.

I will always remember the day he came and got me and took me to live with him. He saw my situation at home, and this kindly man took me in as if I were his own child. He treated me just as well, if not better, than his own child, my stepbrother, who was grown and out on his own. When I moved in, I left home with only the clothes on my back, and he bought me new things. Joe exhibited complete love and compassion for a child who had no one and nowhere else to turn.

Time passed, and I got complacent, as adolescents will do. One day, I got in trouble for possession of marijuana. I was released from the detention center, but not before Joe tried to legally adopt me. At the time, the state said he was too old to do so. So, I was placed on probation for the marijuana charge and sent to a Baptist boarding school out of town.

Unlike the other girls there, I wasn't allowed to come home on weekends. So, to get around that, one weekend I ran away to Joe's when one of the girl's parents came to get her. Joe showed such patience! He called the school and took me back. When I did this a second time, however, the school wouldn't take me back and my probation officer put me back in detention for two weeks.

When I was released to Joe, I was allowed to go to school from his home, and I stayed in school and out of trouble. I was a troubled adolescent and certainly made mistakes, but largely due to Joe's positive influence and his compassion for me, I learned my lesson. Eventually, Joe bought me a car so I could drive myself to school and to my job at a local steak house. I'd passed through my rebellious stage with far fewer problems because of Joe.

I graduated from high school and attended one year of college because Joe had begun saving college funds for me. Then I married, and Joe made a down payment on a house for my new husband and me.

I always wondered if Joe were my real father. I used to ask him all the time if this were true, and he always chuckled and said he wasn't, but that I felt like a real daughter to him. This is what happens when we show others unconditional, compassionate love.

When Joe was dying of cancer, I wondered if he finally might tell me he was my biological father. But I never asked again, and he never said he was. But because of Joe, I learned that there are all kinds of kinships in life—though he always said he wasn't my father, he certainly was a mom, dad, grandmother, and grandfather all in one. He taught me the true meaning of love, the true meaning of compassion. He forever lives in my heart.

So, there's Janet's story, one that can inspire us all about the power of love.

Chapter 5:
Let Christ Show You How to Worship Him

"For God so loved the world that He gave His only Son, so that everyone who believes in Him will not perish but have eternal life." **(John 3:16)**

My dear friend, fill your soul with God's divine love and allow yourself to receive the gift of love freely given to those who believe. When you receive this transfusion of love, you will instantly know it. It's a supernatural feeling that only God can provide.

Jesus died for us—he sacrificed his body for our sins. That's divine love, Godly love. Can you imagine the pain, the agony, the tears, and the blood? Can you picture a mother looking up at her son, bleeding to death, and not being able to do anything to help?

Can you imagine the emotions of that mystical miracle

of a day? Jesus allowed his own body to be the vehicle through which our sins were nailed to the cross that day. He gave up his life, his mother, his friends, his apostles—all for us. He was humble and followed God's will.

Jesus died so we would have eternal life. We know God's way is perfect **(Psalm 18:30)**, for the Word of God is flawless.

This love is an intimate bond. It's a union of our soul with our Father. God *is* love. **(I John 4:8).** God's one true nature is love, just as Jesus's nature was love. In this, the love of God manifested toward us, God sent His only begotten Son into the world, that we might live through Him. In this love, it is not that we loved God, but that He loved us and sent His Son to be the propitiation for our sins. **(I John 4:9–10)**

You see, love means forgiveness. Begin now—why wait? Forgive those who have harmed you, and pray for them—it will please God, and it will bring you so much joy!

We love God because He first loved us. *If someone says, "I love God," yet hates his brother, he is a liar; for he who does not love his brother whom he has seen, how can he love God whom he has not seen? And this commandment we have from Him; that he who loves God must love his brother also."* **(I John 19–21)**

What is the greatest love God has given you today? Well, that's an easy one! God gave you another day, today, and that is the greatest love of all. He gave you one more day to save your soul simply by turning to Him.

So, in all things, give thanks to the Lord, and you will be instantly drawn to His power. Learn to have the mind-set of God. Learn to love as God loves. And always remember: God has infinite wisdom, and He knows how to work with you in your life.

God's Love Brings Peace

Love brings serenity to the soul, a feeling of joyful contentment.

Now hope does not disappoint, because the love of God has been poured out in our hearts by the Holy Spirit who was given to us. (**Romans 5:5**)

Draw upon your soul and lift it up to serve God. There is no higher grace than God's love, and no greater peace. Just offer up your soul to God's height and the peace you've always sought will be attained.

I delight to do your will, O my God, and Your law is within my heart. (**Psalm 40:8**)

But the fruit of the Spirit is love, joy, peace, long suffering, kindness, goodness, faithfulness, gentleness, self-control. Against such there is no law. (**Galatians 5:22–23**)

Jesus said to him, "You shall love the Lord your God with all your heart, with all your soul, and with all your mind. This is the first and great commandment." (**Matthew 22: 37–38**)

"Then you will call upon Me and go and pray to Me, and I will listen to you. And you will seek Me and find Me, when you search for Me with all your heart. I will be found by you, says the Lord, and I will bring you back from your captivity; I will gather you from all the nations and from all the places where I have driven you, says, the Lord, and I will bring you to the place from which I cause you to be carried away captive." (**Jeremiah 29:12–14**)

The Power of Humility

Humility is the key to spiritual freedom. Through personal humility, God will grant you favor. You might be wondering how humble you have to be, especially if you're going through the worst trial of your life. Maybe you believe nothing is going right, so how can you be more humble?

If you can rid your soul of pride and arrogance, and submit to God with a true heart and mind, you will achieve true humility, which holds the key to freedom. Humility means choosing to walk in obedience and submitting to God. It means showing the proper respect for God.

God brings grace, favor, prosperity, blessings, wisdom, and honor to those with a humble spirit, and with the right motive. Humility is the absence of pride and arrogance. Think you can't handle a dose or two of humility? Try these out for size:

- *Let go and let God handle everything.*
- *Have a humble spirit and the right motive.*
- *Have childlike faith.*

Whatever trial you're going through, whatever burden you are carrying, God will free you from it if you believe in Him, and keep a sense of wonder and awe, or a "childlike" faith. I know you may be in an impossible situation, and it seems nothing can be done. However, that's a misconception. The real world and the spiritual world are two different entities. In the real world, your situation may seem impossible. But in the spiritual world, God makes the impossible, possible!

Then Jesus said to the disciples, *"Have faith in God. I assure you that you can say to this mountain, 'May God lift you up and throw you into the sea'; and your command will be obeyed. All that's required is that you really believe and do not doubt in your heart. Listen to me! You can pray for anything, and if you believe, you will have it. But when you are praying, first forgive anyone you are holding a grudge against so that your Father in Heaven will forgive your sins too.* **(Mark 11:22–25)**

God will remove your burdens, trials, or tribulations if you:

- *Believe, trust, and do not doubt.*

- *Pray for your enemies and don't hold grudges.*

- *Have pure motives.*

And we know that God causes everything to work together for the good of those who love God and are called according to His purpose for them. **(Romans 8:28)**

So surrender all your problems to God, and He will move mountains for you! No matter what the mountain is in your life, if you have faith and trust, and your motives are pure, the Lord Jesus will take care of you, and your mountains will disappear.

Whatever burden you are carrying, know that God loves you and He will free you from your burdens if you just believe and have faith. **(Matthew 21:28–30)**

So, stop worrying about your problems—now!

Repeat the following statement three times, and

make it your daily mantra: *I'm going to stop stressing, so I can receive God's blessings.*

Keep it up, and just watch your life change. Give God the freedom He needs to move inside your life, and make it work for the best!

Ten Ways to Keep Your "Humble Meter" in Balance

- ✓ Have a servant-like attitude.
- ✓ Choose God's divine way instead of your way, or what your flesh is telling you to do. Miracles happen when you make the choice to follow God's Word and live under His law, not yours.
- ✓ Trust and depend on God with your heart and soul.
- ✓ Walk in fear of the Lord.
- ✓ Receive undeserved favors.
- ✓ Submit and surrender all control to God, in meekness and humility.
- ✓ Bow down before the Lord when you pray.
- ✓ Honor Jesus Christ. Give him credit for all your work.
- ✓ Train your children to adhere to God's Word.
- ✓ Have a genuine love and caring for all people. When you can see the good in others, this is how you know you have a humble heart.

When you have a humble spirit and the right motive, you will hear from Heaven! How's that for motivation?

God promises that He will hear us when our attitude

is humble and our motives are pure. And remember, it's easier than you may think to keep that humble meter in balance: just let go of pride and arrogance and cast all your worries onto God.

Remember that the devil causes pride, arrogance, worry, and anxiety. So, when you feel threatened or your spirits are low, tell the devil, "I rebuke you in the name of Jesus!" Then stomp him under your feet.

However, it's important to realize that you cannot save yourself—only God can save you. Stay "teachable" and read the Word, and you will grow in God. When you let Jesus live in you, you will get rid of selfishness, anger, and hatred, and almost effortlessly you will find yourself having a forgiving attitude.

Then if My people who are called by My name will humble themselves and pray and seek My face and turn from their wicked way, I will hear from Heaven and forgive their sins and heal their land. **(2 Chronicles 7:14)**

You see, it's in the Word, and the Word is true. If you tell God, "Dear Lord, I need you in my life," He promises healing. Likewise, you younger people must submit yourselves to your elders. Yes, all of you be submissive to one another and be clothed with humility for "*God resists the proud, but gives grace to the humble.*" **(James 4:6)**

Therefore, humble yourselves under the mighty hand of God so that He may exalt you in due time, casting all your cares upon Him, for He certainly cares for you. **(2 Peter 5–11)**

God will give you grace, which is undeserved favor. So, cast all of your worries onto Him.

Enjoy Your Childlike Faith

God wants us to humble ourselves like little children. When I was a little girl, I always depended on my daddy to put groceries on the table. I never worried about not eating, because I knew he'd provide for me. I never worried about my clothes—it didn't even cross my mind. I lived my life as a child without worry, always trusting, forgiving, and loving my father. That is the same kind of relationship God wants us to embrace with Him.

You might ask how and why you should become childlike again.

Matthew 18:1–4 says, *About that time the Disciples came to Jesus and asked, "Which of us is greatest in the Kingdom of Heaven?" Jesus called a small child over to Him and put the child among them. Then He said, "I assure you, unless you turn from your sins and become like little children, you will never get into the Kingdom of Heaven. Therefore, anyone who becomes as humble as this little child is the greatest in the Kingdom of Heaven."*

God wants us to trust and love Him as if we were little children. He wants us to be sincere, to trust in Him, and to be a forgiving person. God will meet your needs and embrace you if you turn to Him with childlike faith. No matter what trial you are going through, trust in the Lord.

We must trust the Lord's direction and His corrective hand. God puts restraints on us so we can be taught correction, and so we will stop repeating our negative actions. Trust in the Lord. It might just be the wrong time in your life for our Lord to calm the storm, but always know that God will work everything out in His timing if you trust Him as if you were a little child, with complete faith.

Prayer

Heavenly Father, I come before you as nothing but the dust from which I was created. I stand before you because I am a sinner in need of your forgiveness, mercy, and grace.

Oh Father, all-powerful, I need you in my life. I surrender and submit all control to you. I cast out all my wicked ways in the name of Jesus. I ask forgiveness of all my sins. I give all obedience to you. I am praying to renew myself. Let not my will be done, but let your will be done. I know you are in control of my life. I know I can do nothing without you.

Dear Lord, obtain for me my petition in this necessity ... [state your petition here]. *Lord, build me and strengthen me and make me into what I ought to be. In the name of Jesus our Lord and Savior, I ask these favors of you. This is a prayer of your faithful servant. Amen.*

Ask God to Open the Door to His House

Do you find yourself in the same situation over and over again? Do you find yourself falling into the same rut? Does your life feel like a revolving door at times?

When you worship the Lord, He will usher you to

the other side! He will be glad to open the door for you! You will feel centered and no longer seem to be running in circles. If you learn to worship and praise Him while you are low, you will be very fruitful and pleasing in God's sight.

Worship means submitting your mind, spirit, body, and soul to the Lord. It means relinquishing all your desires, problems, and wants to the Lord. You can worship the Lord by reading scriptures, praising, singing, receiving communion, and engaging in fellowship. You can worship by private petitions, by public worship, and by offering your body as a Holy Temple to the Lord. We should praise the Lord continually.

Let us continually offer the sacrifice of praise to God; let us give thanks to His name from the fruit of our lips. **(Hebrews 13:15)**

We often find ourselves worshipping the Lord only sporadically, perhaps just in stressful times. We may alienate ourselves from our maker when all is well. Then, when adversity strikes, we become frantic and pray to the Lord, expecting an immediate answer. When He doesn't answer right then, we become impatient, and the Lord becomes the object of our anxiety. It's time to change: it's time to rely on God.

I have joy and peace in my soul because I wake up with the Lord every morning, and I go to sleep with the Lord every night. Negative thoughts don't run through my mind constantly anymore. I continually praise the Lord all day, every day.

Years ago, I found it difficult to go to sleep at night, and I tossed and turned because I couldn't stop thinking about everything I had to do the next day. Some nights,

I had bad dreams. I'd allowed the world to creep in, and in doing so, I'd left God out.

That was then—back before I submitted to the will of God. When I submitted and began to praise God, my life turned around. I prayed and worshipped the Lord until my sleeplessness was completely gone. Today, when I wake up in the morning, I say, "Thank you, Jesus." I'm so excited that God has given me another day. Then I read my Christian devotional, which has a short reading for every day. I spend time looking up the scriptures that correlate with the reading. This only takes a few minutes before work.

Try this quiet time in the morning and your day will be brighter, too. You will feel energized mentally and physically. Spending quiet devotional time causes you to smile more and find more patience amid the tussles of the world. You will really participate in life instead of just going through the motions.

When I'm at work, the restroom is the only quiet place I can find. So I say a short prayer there every day and I hum spiritual songs throughout the day.

I have found truth in the saying, "When you believe, you receive." Praise is our weapon in spiritual warfare against our enemies.

I will be glad and rejoice in You; I will sing praise to Your name, O Most High. When my enemies turn back, they shall fall and perish at Your presence. **(Psalm 9:2–3)**

Sometimes, Satan will try to distract us with worldly things so we will lose our desire to worship God. He'll try to discourage us, making us doubt ourselves and God. Satan will try to make you feel like a failure, and he will make you believe that worshipping God won't do you any good.

Consider the story of Adam and Eve. The devil tricked Eve into sinning by saying, "You surely won't die. You will become just like God, knowing everything, both good and evil." The devil made the temptation great.

When the Lord found out that they'd fallen for Satan's tricks, He said, *"Because you have done this, you are cursed more than all cattle, and more than every beast of the field; on your belly you shall go, and you shall eat dust all the days of your life. And I will put enmity between you and the woman and between your seed and her seed. He shall bruise your head and you shall bruise his heel."* **(Genesis 3:14–15)**

The snake is the lowest form of all animals on Earth. This scripture shows the devil doesn't care how low he has to go to get you. His plan is to win your soul. As long as his attack is effective, he will do anything. He will appeal to every sense, everything sexual. He will get into your thoughts, and he can corrupt your mind within seconds if you are unguarded.

That's why worship is so important! It makes your enemies flee. The movie, *The Passion of the Christ* (produced by Mel Gibson) portrays the true picture of Satan lurking around. He kept letting Jesus know he didn't *have* to go to the cross. He didn't *have* to die for our sins. He was always there, ready to attack, even when it became obvious that Jesus was going to be true to his father.

Satan also lurks around in our lives today. He wants your soul to become tepid. He will move slowly, setting you up, until it's too late. He will catch you off guard.

We may write off little white lies as normal, and soon we think that a harsh word here, a little addiction here, a little gossip here, or a little sex here isn't important. We forget that the devil attacks our minds through our thoughts.

Many people don't understand how educated, successful people end up in jail. It's because their minds become corrupted, and they become greedy. They aren't necessarily bad people—often they are good people who made bad decisions. It's so sad to witness how the devil corrupts people's minds, making them angry and full of vengeance.

So, protect your soul from the devil today. Worship the Lord! Praise His holy name. Learn to praise the Lord when you wake up. Sing praises in the shower. Sing praises on the way to work. Jump up and say "Hallelujah!" Stop right now and sing praise to the Lord! If you don't know a prayer, stand up and lift both of your hands to the Lord and say this one:

Prayer

Thank you, Jesus, Thank you, Lord, I magnify and praise your holy name. Thank you for the sunshine. Thank you for the green in the grass. Thank you for the use of my limbs. Thank you for my breath. Thank you, Jesus. Thank you, Jesus. Lord, my soul says yes to your name. Lord, my soul says yes to your will. Lord, my soul says yes to your Word. Hallelujah, Hallelujah, in Jesus's name I pray. AMEN.

Do you feel better? If not, then repeat this praise over and over until all that unhappiness has left you and you feel the goodness in your soul.

Learn to sing to the Lord. Buy a Christian CD. Life up your voice to the Lord and praise Him. It doesn't matter how you sound—your voice will be beautiful to our Lord!

A burdened heart can't sing, but when you sing, your burdens lift. The Lord loves the praises of His people. When you praise God, worship Him in spirit and in truth.

But the hour is coming, and now is when the true worshippers will worship the Father in spirit and truth, for the Father is seeking such to worship Him. God is spirit, and those who worship Him must worship in spirit and truth. **(John 4:23–24)**

You will find strength and blessings beyond your wildest dreams.

I will praise you with my whole heart; before the gods I will sing praises to you. I will worship toward Your Holy Temple, and praise Your name, for Your loving kindness and Your truth; for You have magnified your word above all Your name. In the day when I cried out, You answered me, and made me bold with strength in my soul. **(Psalm 138:1–3)**

Fifteen Ways to Praise the Lord

> ➤ Lift up your hands in the sanctuary and bless the Lord. **(Psalm 134:2)**

> ➤ Present your bodies as a living and holy sacrifice to the Lord. **(Romans 12:1)**

> ➤ Shout with joy to the Lord. **(Romans 12:1)**

➤ Give thanks to Him and bless His name. **(Psalm 100:4)**

➤ Praise Him for His heavenly dwelling. Praise the Lord!

➤ Praise God in His sanctuary!

➤ Praise Him in His mighty firmament!

➤ Praise Him for His mighty acts!

➤ Praise Him according to His excellent greatness!

➤ Praise Him with the sound of the trumpet!

➤ Praise Him with the lute and harp!

➤ Praise Him with the timbrel and dance!

➤ Praise Him with stringed instruments and flutes!

➤ Praise Him with loud cymbals!

➤ Let everything that has breath praise the Lord!

➤ *Sing to the Lord a new song; sing to the Lord all the Earth.* **(Psalm 96:1)**

➤ Worship in Truth—**(John 4:24)** Worship God according to the truth of God's Word.

➤ Worship in Spirit—**(John 4:24)** *O come, let us worship and bow down: kneel before the Lord our maker.* **(Psalm 95:6)**

➤ Worship with Others—*Where two or three are gathered together in My name, there am I in the midst of them.* **(Matthew 18:20)**

➤ Sing with grace in your hearts. **(Colossians 3:16)**

➤ Worship in silence.

> Praise Him for Holy Spirit. **(Ephesians 6:18)**
> Praise Him with others. **(Hebrews 2:12)**
> Praise Him from your lips. **(Hebrews 13:15)**

Instructions for Worship

For you shall worship no other God, for the Lord, whose name is Jealous, is a jealous God. **(Exodus 34:14)**

You shall love the Lord your God with all your heart, with all your soul, and with all your strength. **(Deuteronomy 6:5)**

Seek the Lord and His strength; seek His face evermore! **(Psalm 105:4)**

"I beseech you therefore, brethren, by the mercies of God, that you present your bodies a living sacrifice, holy, acceptable to God, which is your reasonable service." **(Romans 12:1)**

Finally, brethren, whatever things are true, whatever things are noble, whatever things are just, whatever things are pure, whatever things are lovely, whatever things are of good report, if there is any virtue and if there is anything praiseworthy—meditate on these things. The things which you learned and received and heard and saw in Me, these do, and the God of peace will be with you. **(Philippians 4:8–9)**

Five Good Reasons to Worship

- ✓ To grasp the power of God's presence and power. **(I Corinthians 11:29)**
- ✓ For humility, meekness, and quietness of spirit.
- ✓ For repentance.
- ✓ For mercy, forgiveness and loving kindness.
- ✓ For inner joy.

Judging Others

All of us, regardless or nationality or gender, have an inner, inexplicable longing deep within our souls for love that can only be filled by God. God created this unquenchable desire for love and contentment because He knew that the only way for us to fill this void is to accept Jesus and follow His commandments.

In this life, we have a choice to produce *wholesome fruit* or *rotten fruit*. As our Redeemer is coming to judge us, it's time to change our souls, repent, and be ready for the King's arrival.

We need to come to grips with where we are and where we wish to go. One of the fundamental principles we'll be judged on is how we have treated others. Do you judge people by their weight, color, appearance, or nationality? Have you ridiculed or made fun of people lately? Can you make a list of good deeds you've done in the last month? How many can you come up with? How can you improve that score?

We all have sinned and are in need of reconciliation. When we turn to our maker and repent, we are forgiven. The sins we've committed are forgotten, and our record is expunged. God turns a new page for us and provides a clean slate. We become like a newborn when we experience a spiritual rebirth.

We have the chance, by God's grace alone, to start all over again, as though we've never sinned in the first place! It is a wonderful, fulfilling, and extraordinary feeling, unlike any other on Earth.

As part of our God-given free will, we have a choice to produce wholesome or rotten fruit. The Lord won't smack you upside the head and say, "Hey, pal, I will forgive you if you do this, that, or the other." But even if we make the wrong choice, He forgives our sins, then forgets them because He loves us. It's that simple; it's that pure and true.

Close your eyes and take yourself to Calvary. Look at Jesus hanging on the cross. Look at his arms—they are outstretched. Those arms symbolize his genuine love for us, the love he has within him, the arms with which he wants to embrace us. Those same arms stretched out on the cross will be the same arms that will greet you in Heaven—and the goal is to make it there.

Jesus forgives us. But think about something for a moment: what would happen if he judged you before he decided to forgive you? I'll bet that's a scary thought. And that's exactly how we feel when we judge; we literally block our soul's pathway to Heaven.

Our nation is at war, but even many families are at war. Sadly, we live in a world where many have great animosity toward others who are not "like us." Or, we find fault in others and focus on negativity. Some of us join certain groups, then ostracize those who don't fit in. But if we continue to act with prejudice against others, we fail and become miserable ourselves. And that's no way to get through the gates of Heaven.

Most of us find ourselves teasing or ridiculing others, and we may find gossip entertaining. We know it's wrong, but we do it anyway. But beware: even when it seems like innocent fun, the devil smiles. His plan ruins us and makes us egocentric. Treating others badly stains and mars our souls. The light of our souls grows dim, eventually replaced with darkness.

Declare War Against the Devil!

We can stop our ludicrous behavior. Rather than being at war with each other, we need to be at war with the devil. We should strive to live in harmony with each other, and that means that we stop the gossip and judgment.

When we come together to declare war against Satan, the devil *will* be defeated. God is simply more powerful. We have to persuade ourselves that this spiritual war is worth our lives, our souls. Form an army for the Lord to rebuke and expose evil.

Christ Is the Only Fair Judge!

Christ is the only fair judge—one who has no prejudice. We are all equal in God's eyes. **(Acts 10:28)**

Judge others and you'll be judged yourself. Why would you condemn or look down on another Christian knowing we are all the same in the eyes of God? Each of us will stand personally before the judgment seat of God.

For the scriptures say, "*As surely as I live, says the Lord, every knee will bow to me and every tongue will confess allegiance to God."* **(Romans 14:10–13)**

Peace is the answer to war and conflict. We can find that peace in Jesus. Invite the spirit of God to live in you, and you will receive a new heart and mind.

God helps us live in complete harmony with each other. Through the Lord's power, we can learn to accept all people exactly as they are in their station of life.

Be generous rather than selfish. Be humble, and think about the well-being of others. **(Philippians 2:3–4)**

As we all know, peace and harmony are sorely missing in today's society. Remember Jesus teaches us to love one another as he loved us. **(John 15:12)** Even with all of the negativity, Jesus still has the greatest followers in the world. Why? Because all he asks us to do is love one another and live in peace.

We can use God's spirit living within us to accomplish this. We can draw upon His strength for patience, steadiness, and encouragement. He will satisfy our thirst.

Love with a perpetual love that stands out. Begin to associate with those who you may not normally think of as like-minded. You will find we all have similarities. We all value our friends and family and our church. We are all children of God.

The Lord wants to hear positives. To start producing good fruit, reach out to those you dislike and watch what happens. It's easy to be affable to those we like, but try it with those you dislike. I once saw a man who for some reason had never been very nice to me. When I went out of my way to be nice to him and inquire about his health, he shocked me by returning my courtesy. I felt like God was testing me, and I'd passed the test with flying colors!

I know God put this person in my pathway that day to rid me of the anger and resentment I felt toward him. I realize now this was a test. It was not coincidence—it was divine intervention. So this is yet another reason to never judge others: God may indeed be "testing" you through a message from the Holy Spirit.

Forgive One Another

Challenge your mind to do what is right and forgive one another as Jesus has forgiven you.

You must make allowance for each other's faults and forgive the person who offends you. Remember, the Lord forgave you, so you must forgive others. And the most important piece of clothing you must wear is love. Love is what binds us all together in perfect harmony. And let the peace that comes from Christ rule in your hearts. For as members of one body you are all called to live in peace and always be thankful. **(Colossians 3:13–15)**

Forgive when others have wronged you.

I am warning you! If another believer sins, rebuke him, then if he repents, forgive him. Even if he wrongs you seven times a day and each time turns again and asks forgiveness, forgive him. **(Luke 17:3–4)**

Come together with others. God smiles when folks join together. Do something nice this week. Take someone out to dinner, visit the sick, give money to the poor, or help someone in need.

The prophet Isaiah foretold the Savior's coming. He was disgusted because of the level of sin and corruption in Jerusalem during the Babylonian exile of 587 BC.

Isaiah told the people that the spirit of the Lord would rest upon Jesus. **(Isaiah 11:2)** The spirit would give Jesus wisdom, knowledge, understanding, and fear of the Lord. Isaiah told the people that the Messiah would judge them by fairness and truth. He preached to the people to get along with each other because the Messiah was coming to offer salvation.

His prophecy came true: Jesus came and offered salvation to all of us by dying for our sins. And He will return again to judge us. But do not judge yourself … and remember the golden rule: treat others as you would want to be treated.

A sure way to produce good fruit is to stay on the vine, with Jesus Christ. **(John 15:1–8)**

The Scriptures Tell Us How to Produce Good Fruit

If someone says, "I love God," and hates his brother, he is a liar; for he who does not love his brother whom he has seen, how can he love God whom he has not seen? **(I John 4:20)**

Be kindly affectionate to one another with brotherly love, in honor giving preference to one another. **(Romans 12:10)**

But I say to you, love your enemies, bless those who curse you, do good to those who hate you, and pray for those who spitefully use you and persecute you, that you may be sons of your Father in Heaven; for He makes His sun rise on the evil and on the good, and sends rain on the just and on the unjust. For if you love those who love you, what reward have you? Do not even the tax collectors do the same? **(Matthew 5:44–46)**

And this commandment we have from Him; that he who loves God must love his brother also. **(I John 4:21)**

And the second is like it; you shall love your neighbor as yourself. **(Matthew 22:39)**

Let nothing be done through selfish ambition or conceit, but in lowliness of mind let each esteem others better than himself. **(Philippians 2:3)**

The Balance of Giving and Receiving

I love to give Christmas gifts. I always search for the perfect gift for each family member until everyone has the perfect Christmas present. But it used to be that then I'd see something else, something that I thought was better, and I'd buy that present also. This meant going overboard, and now I realize my doing so came from my need to outdo everyone. I gave others the kinds of gifts that would bring attention directly upon me. But I never realized this until I started to depend on God.

God can humble you and make you see the dangerous waters you're navigating. God showed me that a fundamental principle of giving and receiving is the *balance* found between the two.

I hadn't understood that the object of the gift is us. We often give because of the attention the act of giving receives.

We see this during the holidays when a whole lot of debt is accumulated. We can almost smell the plastic credit cards in the mall. We're seduced into the store by so many messages that tell us to buy, buy, buy. The need to stand out and be the top giver becomes an obsession, an addiction, a demon—like crack cocaine. It doesn't matter how much money it takes, we want to be the top giver.

Too often, we give our children whatever they want and don't think about what message we're sending. We may buy things ready-made that our children could make for themselves. We buy the make-believe house rather than giving children the cardboard or blocks to build it themselves. Rather than fostering creativity and imagination, we may stunt their growth. We also may not persuade our children to work for what they want, and that makes them unappreciative and even lazy.

We need to adopt a divine perspective and change the object of our giving. Christmas is not about honoring each other, but about honoring God. We honor God through Christ, whom He has given us. And the gift that you get from God is everlasting life.

Before Jesus Christ, we were all cut off from God. God sent Jesus to open that door to Him. He sent us a gift, His Son. So now, when our praises go up, blessings come down upon us. That's what Christmas is all about.

If you've ever been lost, then you know that the minute you recognize you don't know where you are, you seek the right path. When you want salvation and deliverance but you don't know the way, seek the Lord and He will show you the way, just as his Word says.

Ask, and it will be given to you; seek, and you will find; knock, and it will be opened to you. For everyone who asks receives, and he who seeks finds, and to him who knocks it will be opened. **(Matthew 7:7–8 NKJV)**

Sometimes, we are so lost that even though we see salvation, we can't get up and claim it! We see miracles and blessings all around us. We see others rejoicing, but we aren't so happy because it's not about us. How do you expect God to bless you when you continue to see everything as being about me, myself, and I? You should rejoice when others receive blessings. Praise God for the blessings of others. It's the basic principle of giving and receiving.

You may know that the government stockpiles food, but when the warehouses are full, they give food away. If the government didn't give away these commodities, they would have no place to store all the new stockpiles of food. This principle correlates to us: if you aren't giving, you get too full to receive!

My closets are full. If I want to receive blessings, I must get rid of the stockpiles in my closet. This applies to both literal closets and spiritual closets. We keep piling our spiritual closets with stuff, stuff, and more stuff. Have you thought about how much less complicated your life would seem, how much lighter your load would feel, if you took some of this stuff out? What would you take out? Would it be bitterness, attitude, stubbornness, pride, selfishness, anger, and addiction? Clean your closet and get rid of all that junk!

Give back all the wrongs in your life, and then receive the best gift there ever was. Give yourself to Jesus—he's waiting for our gift! The Wise Men didn't give gifts to each other, and they didn't rejoice in each other. They gave gifts to Jesus Christ.

So, the next time you can't afford extravagant gifts, give the gift of praise. "I don't have much for you in the way of material goods," you can say, "but hallelujah, sister!" Give a Bible verse. Show the key to eternal life, the gift we all desire deep down in the depths of our soul.

Gifts and giving should glorify God. The greatest gift

from God is eternal life. Clean out your closet so you can receive this gift … the greatest treasure of all!

Give Compassion

If a brother or sister is naked, destitute, and deprived of daily food, and one of you says to the person, "Depart in peace, be warmed and filled," but you do not give them the things which are needed for the body, what does it profit? (**James 2:15, 16 NKJV**)

I beseech you therefore, brethren, by the mercies of God, that you present your bodies a living sacrifice, wholly acceptable to God, which is your reasonable service. (**Romans 12:1 NKJV**)

Then everyone came whose heart was stirred, and everyone whose spirit was willing, and they brought the Lord's offering for the work of the tabernacle of meeting, for all its service, and for the holy garments. (**Exodus 35:21 NKJV**)

Then the King will say to those on His right hand, "Come, you blessed of My Father, inherit the kingdom prepared for you from the foundation of the world, for I was hungry and you gave Me food; I was thirsty and you gave Me drink; I was a stranger and you took Me in; I was naked and you clothed Me; I was sick and you visited Me; I was in prison and you came to Me." (**Matthew 25 NKJV**)

Then the righteous will answer Him saying, "Lord, when did we see You hungry and feed You, or thirsty and give You drink? When did we see You a stranger and take You in, or naked and clothe You? Or when did we see You sick, or in prison, and come to You?" And the King will answer and say to them, "Assuredly, I say to you, inasmuch as you did it

to one of the least of these, My brethren, you did it to Me."
(Matthew 25:34–40 NKJV)

*Then Zacchaeus stood and said to the Lord, "Look,
Lord, I give half of my goods to the poor; and if I have taken
anything from anyone by false accusation, I restore fourfold.*
(Luke 19:8 NKJV)

*So let each one give as he purposes in his heart, not
grudgingly or of necessity; for God loves a cheerful giver.* **(II
Corinthians 9:7 NKJV)**

*Honor the Lord with your possessions. And with the first
fruits of all your increase.* **(Proverbs 3:9 NKJV)**

Prayer

*Father, giving in a blessed way does not
always come naturally to me. I know that
we receive to give. (**Matthew 10:8**) Help
me to share your love for the welfare and
happiness of others. Thank you for blessing
me and counting me as a blessing. (**Genesis
12:2**) Lord, help me to give with an inner
love which can only come from your grace.
Help me to be compassionate like the Good
Samaritan. (**Luke 10:30–37**) Help me
to give to you through my enemies, needy
people, and the church. When I give, let
me realize that I should only give to glorify
you. Dear Lord, please help me to cheerfully
give with your light and radiance shining
through me.*

Chapter 6:
Choosing God's Will for Your Life

I am blessed to be alive, because God saved "a wretch like me." If He saved me, He definitely can save you. I'm a living witness of what God can do. At one time, a gross injustice was done to me, and God saved me and gave me favor. God reached down, saved me, cleansed me, and told me all is forgiven. It doesn't matter what you think of me—God has forgiven me, and that's all that matters.

God can do the same for you. All you have to do is accept Him, and He will bless you abundantly. Jesus came to give life. Choose life and begin to enjoy abundant life without fear of what problems or obstacles or hardships you'll face.

In 1999, so many people were scared. Millions and millions of dollars were made on fear from sales of food, batteries, candles, and even underground shelters. Yet Y2K, the year 2000, came and went, and nothing bad happened.

What does this tell you? It tells us that what man fears doesn't frighten God. This fear of the turn of the century was created from an illusion with too many of us being afraid that computers would collapse. This fear was pumped up through TV, radio, and newspapers. Yet, it was an illusion, like so many of our personal fears. It also came from our not trusting and having faith in God. We can rest easy, knowing that whatever comes up, God has created us and made us what we are, and He will always protect us.

But by the grace of God I am what I am, and His grace toward me was not in vain; but I labored more abundantly than they all, yet not I, but the grace of God which was with me. **(I Corinthians 15:10 NKJV)**

So, no matter what you are going through, go through it knowing God will protect you. Fear not.

For You, O Lord, will bless the righteous; with favor You will surround Him as with a shield. **(Psalm 5:12 NKJV)**

Walk with your shoulders back and your head high, knowing that God has already resolved whatever problems you may have encountered—or will encounter in the future.

Repeat this to yourself: "I will not be a victim! I will have victory!"

God has already orchestrated how man would come back to Him. Although it is hard to fathom, 9/11 was part of His master plan. When that horrific event occurred, those who put their faith in God managed to rise above the fear and chaos and inner peace took over.

Remember, the devil always sets traps for us. You have to listen to the little voice in your head, the one that tells you, "Don't go there, don't do that." Listen to that voice—it's your conscience speaking, coming directly from God. On the other hand, the devil always comes to attack. Have no fear, because fear is a tool and a trick of the devil.

God's grace helps you overcome fear. God gives us the ability to go on when we can no longer go on alone—and we don't ever need to feel alone.

We need hope and we need encouragement. God will give it to us because He loves us. His love will cast out all of our fear.

There is no fear in love, but perfect love casts out fear, because fear involves torment. But he who fears has not been made perfect in love. **(I John 4:18 NKJV)**

God is the ruler of our lives. Turn everything over to Him and He will work it out. Grace is unmerited favor and was given to us when He extended His arms and through his Son, Jesus Christ, died on the cross. It's your decision to accept it or reject it.

By God's grace, we are protected. God can only give grace to us. Jesus purchased favor for us with God when he died for our sins. This gift, when received, will give us supernatural favor.

Let us therefore come boldly to the throne of grace, that we may obtain mercy and find grace to help in time of need. **(Hebrews 4:16 NKJV)**

For He made Him who knew no sin to be sin for us, that we might become the righteousness of God in Him. **(II Corinthians 5:21 NKJV)**

God gives us mercy. He forgave the thief on the cross,

as He forgives us. All you have to do is ask. *Ask* for His favor—He is waiting to give it to you. Just receive it. It's like a Christmas present. If I have a present for you, and I reach toward you with it in my hand, you must stretch your hands out to receive it.

Let God's grace reign in your life. Understand you don't have to work for it—it's yours for the asking.

I received favor when I opened my business, as it became very successful, and it seemed the business flocked to me. But I knew it wasn't all my doing;

I also asked for God's favor when writing this book. What favor do you need? Of course, you can always ask a friend for a favor. But guess what? Friends can always say no.

So, enjoy God's favor all by yourself. Nobody can take this favor from you.

You therefore, My son, be strong in the grace that is in Christ Jesus. **(II Timothy 2:1 NKJV)**

But grow in the grace and knowledge of our Lord and Savior, Jesus Christ. **(II Peter 3:18 NKJV)**

Grace to you and peace from God Our Father and the Lord Jesus Christ. **(Ephesians 1:2 NKJV)**

Then He gave him the covenant of circumcision; and so Abraham begot Isaac and circumcised him on the eighth day; and Isaac begot Jacob, and Jacob begot the twelve patriarchs. And the patriarchs, becoming envious, sold Joseph into Egypt. But God was with him and delivered him out of all his troubles, and gave him favor and wisdom in the presence of Pharaoh, King of Egypt; and he made him governor over Egypt and all his house. **(Acts 7:8–10 NKJV)**

Prayer

Dear heavenly Father, illuminate my mind. Illuminate my heart. Reveal to me what you have done for me. I need victory. I know that victory was given to me on the cross at Calvary. Renew my faith, Lord. Renew my joy. Let me hear you calling me. Thank you, Lord, for being there through the mist of fear, confusion, and chaos in my life. Thank you for being there for me even when I was in rebellion. Thank you for not leaving me. Thank you for your divine rulership. Undress me, Lord. Strip me and wash me, so I will be as white as snow. Wash me, Lord; redeem me, Lord; and restore me, Lord. Let me see all my flaws and mistakes, Lord. Let thy favor rest with me.

[name your favor here]. *We give you glory, Lord. We bless Your name. Alleluia. I praise you Lord, for all the blessings you have given me in the past. I glorify you, Lord. I feel at peace now, Lord, because I know my blessing is on the way. Alleluia, Alleluia. In Jesus's name we pray. Amen.*

When I let my emotions bring me down, I find I feel like a hypocrite because I know they shouldn't affect my faith. However, I remember back to the time I turned my will over to Christ. I put all my problems, worries, anger, and family difficulties into God's hands. I stopped worrying about all the facets of my life because I knew our God had a plan for me. I knew He would work it out. I understood that His thoughts were higher than my thoughts. I knew without a shadow of a doubt that God was a sovereign God, a truthful God, a caring God, and a faithful God. God was in control.

If I really had given it all to God, why was I setting human standards? I kept giving my will to God, then taking it back. I reasoned with myself, saying, "Well, I have to be realistic here."

When I finally relinquished my will to God, I knew in my heart that I wanted His will to be done in my life. I've learned to have faith in God in all things, for He will work it out. Hope for a miracle—know it can and will happen! It's His will I want, not mine. It's His plan I want worked out in my life.

I know that I'm here for a very special purpose, and it's no accident. I'm here to share Jesus Christ with you. God is working in my life, cleansing my soul and restoring my faith. He has made me righteous. I know He loves me, and I trust His corrective hand. Above all I know, *Eye has not seen, nor ear heard, nor have entered into the heart of man. The things which God has prepared for those who love Him.* (**I Corinthians 2:9 NKJV**)

I know God wanted me to write this book and let others read it. A little voice kept telling me, "Get up and write, Get up and write." I fought it for months. Then, one morning the words started flowing in my mind. Paragraphs started forming. Ideas started popping. I knew the Holy Spirit was telling me to get up and write. But did I finally do it? No—I lay there fighting God's will. I couldn't write a book. Who was I? "Nothing without God," the little voice answered. Still I ignored it and went to sleep.

Have you ever heard a voice telling you something? Did you listen, or just turn a deaf ear? I was running from a call. I was like Jonah, and God had definitely put me in the belly of the whale for a reason. I was running and running. Then God touched me.

What is your calling? Are you running from it? What is God's plan for your life? What will your choice be: God's will or your will?

We are all born with freedom of choice. We may choose good, which is of God, or evil, which is of the devil. We can't mix the two. Light cannot mix with darkness; sin cannot mix with holiness. Our God does not tolerate evil. Evil is being separated from God.

You shall not have in your bag differing weights, a heavy and a light. You shall not have in your house differing measures, a large and a small. You shall have a perfect and just weight, a perfect and just measure, that your days may be lengthened in the land which the Lord your God is giving you. For all who do such things, all who behave unrighteously, are an abomination to the Lord your God. (**Deuteronomy 25:13–16 NKJV**)

I realized when I started worrying that I was giving in to the devil. I knew God wouldn't be happy with my swaying in and out of this kind of anxiousness. Then, I finally realized all of this was a true test of my faith.

The Lord tests the righteous. But the wicked and the one who loves violence, His soul hates. (**Psalm 11:5 NKJV**)

God's original plan was for us *not* to know evil. However, His plan was interrupted by Adam and Eve. But instead of leaving us all doomed to Hell, He gave us mercy. God gave us mercy, and plans to restore us to what we were before Adam and Eve sinned.

But when the fullness of the time had come, God sent forth His Son, born of a woman, born under the law, to redeem those who were under the law, that we might receive the adoption as sons. **(Galatians 4:4–5 NKJV)**

God sent His Son to be a live sacrifice for us. His death would cleanse us from all our sins. He would bridge the gap of separation that Adam and Eve formed.

There is therefore now no condemnation to those who are in Christ Jesus, who do not walk according to the flesh, but according to the Spirit. For the law of the Spirit of life in Christ Jesus has made me free from the law of sin and death. **(Romans 8:1–2 NKJV)**

He came to give us a choice: a choice to choose eternal life.

For the wages of sin is death, but the gift of God is eternal life in Christ Jesus our Lord. **(Romans 6:23 NKJV)**

Acceptance of His will grants eternal life.

That if you confess with your mouth the Lord Jesus and believe in your heart that God has raised Him from the dead, you will be saved. **(Romans 10:9 NKJV)**

If you want God's plan to work in your life, you must accept Jesus Christ.

And I will pray to the Father, and He will give you another Helper, that He may abide with you forever. **(John 14:16 NKJV)**

Chapter 7:
What is God's Plan?

God's plan is simple: we are vehicles for God, and we all have a purpose, which we can find if we truly dig deep and seek it. God wants all of us to be with Him, to walk with Him. He wants us to have eternal life and go to live with Him in Heaven.

"In My Father's house are many mansions; if it were not so, I would have told you. I go to prepare a place for you. And if I go and prepare a place for you, I will come again and receive you to Myself; that where I am, there you may be also." **(John 14:2, 3 NKJV)**

The only way this can happen is for us to accept Jesus Christ and his will.

But there shall by no means enter it anything that defiles, or causes an abomination or a lie, but only those who are written in the Lamb's Book of Life. **(Revelation 21:27 NKJV)**

Listen for the inner voice, as it will show you God's way and His will. Listen for the quiet, still voice. Follow His lead.

Your ears shall hear a word behind you saying, "This is the way, walk in it." Whenever you turn to the right hand, or whenever you turn to the left. **(Isaiah 30:21 NKJV)**

I finally picked up the pen and started to write. I wrote and wrote until I couldn't write any more. Then I lay down until the words started flowing again.

We all have a choice. I could have ignored this little voice. I could have written it off and continued to make excuses, but I didn't. Instead, I decided to accept God's will and His plan for me. I learned not to let my emotions change my will, and I said a little prayer:

Prayer

Dear Lord, I want my will to be the same as your will. I know following your will is not easy, and my emotions will try to deter me. Lord, grant me self-control to control these emotions. I die to myself and I take your side, Dear Lord. In Jesus's name I pray. Amen.

When I began listening to the voice and following God's will, I began to be delivered.

And do not be conformed to this world, but be transformed by the renewing of your mind, that you may prove what is that good and acceptable and perfect will of God. **(Romans 12:2 NKJV)**

I never aspired to be a writer. I was a businesswoman, a microbiologist, and a chemist. But sometimes, for our own good, God puts us in situations we can't understand. Instead of trying to always do our will, we need to do His will—conform our will to His will and our desires to His desires.

I knew a very special lady once named Gloria. She was married to an abusive man who worked for a government agency. She tried to get a divorce, but she couldn't find any attorney who would take her case out of fear of retaliation from her husband and the agency he worked for. In other words, they feared harassment. Sure enough, when Gloria finally found an attorney in Washington who would handle her divorce, her husband managed to send the IRS to harass Gloria's brother, who he didn't like. Gloria was concerned for the safety of herself and her daughters. Here is her testimony to me during her times of trouble:

> *Dear Shawn,*
>
> *This letter has been delayed because I needed time to think about my testimony. This is a hard one for me, as I am not very good with expressing myself. I can talk up a storm one-on-one, but speaking in a group scares me to death. And for some reason, I have not had much courage with sharing my testimony. But here goes ...*
>
> *I think that I first really knew God was with me always in January of 1989. For some reason, I was drawn to read through the Bible in a year. I had purchased one of*

those Bibles that help you do it. I started and then could not put the Bible down. I went way ahead of the planned schedule and finished it in a very short time. I didn't get much sleep, but I gained a closeness to God that I had not had in a long time. I always knew that I was God's child, but had let the intimacy slip away. At this time, I wrote a letter to my girls and copied every Bible verse that I thought was important concerning them loving each other and taking care of each other. It was like I thought that I would not be there for them anymore and they needed to depend on each other. I was on a mission and could not stop. I think that I was being made stronger for what was going to happen in our lives in a few months.

In the fall, the two girls and I left home with very little and started to rebuild new lives. I went through several terrible years in court trying to get a divorce and property settlement. Things were just unbelievable,

At this time, I didn't want the girls out of my sight. They were both seniors; one was in high school and one was in college. One night, I got on my knees and asked God to take care of them as I was not capable of doing it any more. I just opened one tight fist and said, "I give Stephanie to you, God." Then slowly I opened the other fist and said, "I give Allison to you, God." Believe it or not, I had a calm come over me and I had total peace. That was just the most awesome feeling. Can you believe that by giving the girls back totally to God was the only way I could feel secure about them? They always belonged to God, and I knew that, but I had thought that I could protect them myself. How vain I was about my capabilities of being in control.

God has always been with me. I just wasn't as tuned in to Him as He has been to me. Christians can be joyful in tough times because God's purpose is always greater than any other purpose. We just have to line our lives up with His purpose. "A life devoted to things is a dead life, a stump; a God-shaped life is a flourishing tree." (Proverbs 11:28)

This is very interesting that you are writing a book about God's love. I have great plans myself, and I just don't always get finished with what I want to do.

I want you to know that you are in my prayers along with all of your family.

Gloria struggled for many years. However, she asked God for safety and protection, and that's what God delivered. She also asked God to deliver her, and He did. God is our deliverer. **(Psalm 70:5)**

Gloria asked the Lord to be her hiding place. The Lord hid her carefully. **(Psalm 32:7)** Gloria needed God to be her husband. He was her husband. **(Isaiah 54:5)**

Gloria asked the Lord for strength, and her request was granted. The Lord is our strength. **(Psalm 43:2)**

What do you need the Lord to be for you? Whether it's your strength, comforter, provider, healer, friend, or all of the above, all you need to do is ask the Lord for His will to be done in your life, and He will be whatever you need Him to be.

Gloria surrendered her will to the Lord. She trusted the Lord. She gave up her will and replaced it with the higher living will of God.

Gloria's divorce was finalized at last. Her estranged husband had made her life, and that of her brothers and sisters, a living hell. Nothing much ever came from all the investigations of this evil man. But the family was emotionally drained and teamed up and prayed for deliverance. At some later point, her ex-husband developed terminal cancer at a very early age, and he died. Of course, no one would say that God gave the man cancer, but on a personal level, his death came as a great relief. She and her family had already received her deliverance just by asking for God's help and giving each other support.

Now Gloria feels safe. She knew that God's will was for her good. She now teaches Bible studies and leads others through adversity to the Lord, because she wants others to know the Lord as she does. Her adversity had a purpose: it brought glory to God.

Following God's will isn't always easy. When we put our trust in God, the Holy Spirit seals us with a promise of salvation.

In Him you also trusted, after you heard the word of truth, the gospel of your salvation; in whom also, having

believed; you were sealed with the Holy Spirit of promise.
(Ephesians 1:13 NKJV)

Trusting in God helps us develop patience. During trials and tribulations, we are forced to build up true patience. When we trust in the Lord and show Him our faith and love, patience will come.

Knowing that the testing of your faith produces patience.
(James 1:3 NKJV)

And not only that, but we also glory in tribulations, knowing that tribulation produces perseverance. **(Romans 5:3 NKJV)**

For we all stumble in many things. If anyone does not stumble in word, he is a perfect man, able also to bridle the whole body. **(James 3:2 NKJV)**

Dear friend, do an inventory of your life. Say out loud, "Everything in my life is just as it ought to be because I have done everything to make it so."

Do you see the pride, the ego, in this statement? Has your life been perfect? I know it hasn't if you haven't turned and surrendered all to Jesus Christ.

Free Yourself

Acknowledge that you have been your own stumbling block. Only after you acknowledge this can the blocks be moved. Sometimes we stand in our own way. During the adversity in my life, I had major problems, catastrophes, and losses. When I decided to surrender and give it all up to God, I began to be delivered. When I listened to God's call and picked up the pen to start writing, I realized I had let go of my stumbling blocks.

I cannot do this for you—you have to do it for

yourself. Take an inventory and ask God for His will to be done. Give all your cares to Jesus.

Casting all your care upon Him, for He cares for you. **(I Peter 5:7 NKJV)**

It doesn't matter what spiritual shape you are in. Wherever you are, ask God to make you into what you ought to be. Tell God you want His plan to be worked out in your life. God will bring you to an expected end. If you follow God's will, you may not always live better here on Earth, but you will have eternal life.

However, walking with God may be uncomfortable. You may have to bend and twist in ways that sometimes feel uncomfortable or unfamiliar to you. Ask the Lord to give you strength in all uncomfortable situations. For the Lord says, *For His anger is but for a moment, His favor is for life; weeping may endure for a night, but joy comes in the morning.* **(Psalm 30:5 NKJV)**

God loves all of us. His will and His plan are available to everybody. God invites everyone to the Kingdom of Heaven!

And the Spirit and the bride say, "Come!" And let him who hears say, "Come!" And let him who thirsts come. Whoever desires, let him take the water of life freely. **(Revelation 22:17 NKJV)**

Accept your calling. Accept your invitation. Accept Jesus Christ as your Savior, and receive all he has planned for you.

Praise the Lord when you are happy—and when you are sad. You'll never feel like a hypocrite again.

How to Recognize God's Plan for Your Life

(1) *Trust it*—we *must* trust God. Lack of trust leads to stress. Trust wipes out all fear. You can trust God for both small problems and large problems. Trusting God is a part of faith. However, when we don't trust God, we don't receive the best from God. **(Hebrews 3:15–19)** Whenever God's plan is put in front of you, you should trust God. Then you should be willing to follow His plan.

If anyone wills to do His will, he shall know concerning the doctrine, whether it is from God or whether I speak on my own authority. **(John 7:17 NKJV)**

(2) *Test it*—if you aren't sure if God wants something in your life, test it. Is it scriptural? Whatever is scriptural is part of God's plan. For example: if you are praying for a relationship to work out, and the person wasn't sent by God, it's not God's plan. So if you are in love with a married man or woman and you are praying that he or she will leave his or her spouse, then that is not part of God's plan. Use common sense and scriptural references. The Holy Bible is often referred to as the "Catalog of Life." So go shopping! If it is found in the Catalog of Life, it's part of God's plan. If it's not, it's not part of His plan. Such a simple analogy, but truthful simplicity! God's Word is the truth. Find His plan for your life. Go shopping today in the "Catalog of Life."

I will meditate on your precepts, and contemplate your ways. **(Psalm 119:15 NKJV)**

Your word is a lamp to my feet and a light to my path. **(Psalm 119:105 NKJV)**

(3) *Is it only worldly?* If you are in love with worldly possessions, then it is not part of God's will. Worldly

items are desires of the flesh as reflected in things, such as pornography, sexual and other physical desires, material possessions, etc. Deny your flesh. Learn the difference between loving the Father and loving the world.

Do not love the world or the things in the world. If anyone loves the world, the love of the Father is not in him. For all this is in the world, the lust of the flesh, the lust of the eyes, and the pride of life—is not of the Father but is of the world. And the world is passing away, and the lust of it; but he who does the will of God abides forever. **(I John 2:15–17 NKJV)**

(4) *Do you feel it is wrong?* Trust your conscience. If your conscience makes you doubt what you are doing, then don't do it. It's that simple. Also, remember that something that is right for others may not be right for you. God has a different plan for all of us.

Do you have faith? Have it in yourself before God. *Happy is he who does not condemn himself in what he approves. But he who doubts is condemned if he eats because he does not eat from faith; for whatever is not from faith is sin.* **(Romans 14:22, 23 NKJV)**

(5) *Is it pleasing?* God has a perfect plan for all of us. This plan was predestined before the world began. We are not of the world, but of the divine. Persevere in doing God's will, and goodness will follow you all the days of your life.

And do not be conformed to this world, but be transformed by the renewing of your mind, that you may prove what is that good and acceptable and perfect will of God. **(Romans 12:2 NKJV)**

Don't participate in worldly deeds that result in sin. Stay clear of sin, such as sexual sins, greed, lust, foul language, lying, anger, malicious behavior, shameful desires, and violence. Godly behavior means showing kindness, love, humility, patience, and forgiveness. Rebuke evil in the name of Jesus—and stay clear of it. God's will should always be done in the name of Jesus.

And whatever you do in word or deed, do all in the name of the Lord Jesus, giving thanks to God the Father through Him.

And whatever you do, do it heartily; as to the Lord and not to men. **(Colossians 3:17, 23 NKJV)**

Follow God's plan for your life—He that seeketh findeth. **(Matthew 7:8)**

Follow His steps. **(I Peter 2:21)**

Twenty-Five Names for Our God!

1) Wonderful Counselor **(Isaiah 9:6)**
2) Everlasting Father **(Isaiah 9:6)**
3) Prince of Peace **(Isaiah 9:6)**
4) The Redeemer **(Isaiah 59:20)**
5) Good Master **(Matthew 19:16)**
6) The Door **(John 10:7)**
7) The Way, The Truth, The Life **(John 14:6)**
8) The True Vine **(John 15:1)**
9) The Holy One and The Just **(Acts 3:14)**
10) The Chief Cornerstone **(Ephesians 2:20)**
11) The Righteous Judge **(II Timothy 4:8)**
12) High Priest **(Hebrews 10:21)**
13) Author and Finisher of our Faith **(Hebrews 12:2)**
14) Savior **(II Peter 2:20)**
15) Alpha and Omega, The Beginning and The End **(Revelation 1:8)**

16) King of Kings and Lord of Lords **(Revelation 19:16)**
17) Healer **(Psalm 103:3)**
18) Deliverer **(Psalm 70:8)**
19) My Strength **(Psalm 43:2)**
20) Hope **(Psalm 71:5)**
21) My Shield **(Psalm 144:2)**
22) Spirit of Truth **(John 16:13)**
23) Friend **(John 15:15)**
24) Advocate **(I John 2:1)**
25) Love **(I John 4:16)**

And these are just a few of the hundreds of wonderful names assigned to God that are found in the Bible!

Prayer

Dear Lord,

I love you. Let your will be my will. I surrender myself to you. I put all my hardships and losses in your hands. I receive the gift of your Son and I receive you **(I John 2:23)**. *I never want to be separated from you again* **(Romans 8:38–39)**. *I thank you, Lord, for calling me to share in your divine life and your divine plan. In fulfillment of your will, Jesus died on the cross. Jesus gave Himself up to destroy sin and death. I now, Lord, give myself up to you. I no longer want to live for myself, but for your will only.*

Encourage me, Lord, to seek your will **(2 Thessalonians 2:16–17)** *and to serve you. I will listen for your calling and will conform my will to your will. Emotions,* *trials, and tribulations will not deter me. I stand grounded in faith and love, and I surrender my body, mind, and soul to you, dear Lord.*

*Form and mold me, Lord, into the perfect vessel so I can carry out Your plan on Earth. Grant me the endurance needed to receive your blessing for following your will (**Hebrews 10:6**). Accept my sacrifice, dear Lord. I give up all worldly desires and control. I put everything in your hands, Lord. Lord, direct my steps (**Jeremiah 10:23**) and bring me into your divine plan. I ask this in the name of Jesus Christ, our Lord, I pray. Amen.*

Releasing Anger and Resentment

I've worked hard my entire life. At the age of fifteen, I landed my first job at McDonald's. Then from there, I worked at Popeye's, a pizza place, an Exxon station, and a doctor's office. Through college, I had three jobs: waiting tables at Chili's, telemarketing, and cashiering at a gas station. I felt that I missed out on part of my childhood and early adulthood due to my need to work. In turn, I ended up resenting my parents.

I put myself through college. I purchased a mobile home for $2,000, which my grandfather, uncle, and father remodeled.

I remember studying at Chili's between orders, and starving many nights because I didn't have a dollar to my name. I was barely making it. During my freshman and sophomore years, it wasn't that hard. However, going for a degree in microbiology and chemistry meant undertaking a demanding curriculum in the last two years.

In my junior year, I was taking organic chemistry, physics, statistics, and other monstrously difficult classes. By this time, working was out of the question. I needed support, help, and love, but I didn't think they were available. I remember lying in bed one night. It was freezing inside my trailer, and I was so cold. All I had was a portable, plug-in heater. I put my hands around my head, covering my ears. My head was so cold, I squeezed it all night. I'll never forget that night, when I almost froze to death. It was indescribably horrible.

I started harboring resentment toward my parents. Where were they? Why couldn't they buy me a heater? My brothers were in high school and wearing Giraud jeans. I was in college, freezing and starving to death. My brothers barely worked, yet they were given more than I was.

My feelings of resentment grew over the years. When I went to visit my mom, she let me clean out her pantry. I was limited to canned goods because I didn't have a stove. I chose mostly beans—red beans, white beans, navy beans, black-eyed peas—and corn. This was all I ate every day for years. I remember rushing home and eating a can of Blue Runner red beans and crackers. I had to count pennies for gasoline, and a luxury was a Taco Bell bean burrito with lettuce for 69 cents.

During my senior year in college, my $40 electric bill was due. I asked my mother to lend me the money until I received my paycheck, but she refused. "If you lived at home," she said, "you wouldn't have those problems. You chose not to live here."

I cried and cried. I would have liked to live at home, but I couldn't study there because it was always too loud and full of people for me to be able to concentrate. A friend loaned me the money to pay the bill, so I was helped. Still layers and layers of resentment against my parents continued to build. I was angry and miserable.

My parents weren't rich, but they weren't poor, either. They said they couldn't afford to help me, but I never understood or believed that. Although they never gave me one dollar toward my college tuition, they threatened to disown me if I didn't let them claim me on their income tax.

I detached myself from my parents and went home only on holidays—and I didn't feel accepted or welcomed, although I didn't express these feelings to my family. As I matured and got married, my parents started to show more love. However, by then I resented them so much, I couldn't see it.

I know my family realized they were wrong. My dad tells me often that he is saving for his grandchildren to go to college because he didn't send his own children.

I was the first and only one in the family at that time to graduate from college. Slowly, after I got a job and started my professional career, my resentment turned to a quiet kind of pride and belief in myself. I began to realize that my parents' strictness had led to my drive and success. My parents are proud of me today. I wanted a good life for myself, and I was willing to persevere to get it.

Like most children, I had expectations for my parents, and when they didn't meet my expectations, I became resentful. When resentment turned to anger, I found myself miserable. Were my parents miserable? No,

I was the only one, because I was the person who felt detached.

One day, I realized that I would never be able to get my parents to pay for anything because that was their belief system. They grew up in different times and simply believed that at age eighteen, a child is on his or her own. My expectations were clearly an illusion I had created!

I decided (because it is a choice, after all) to accept my parents and let go of anger, resentment, and bitterness. And oddly, it was really only then that I realized my parents truly loved me. I realized that although I *felt* they always loved my brothers more, that was just another of my failed illusions. The devil was trying hard to win my soul, but I gave my soul to God. Then, when I finally let go of all anger, resentment, and bitterness, the devil lost another battle.

I never understood what my parents were trying to do by being so harsh. But whatever the reason, I accepted it, and I accepted them for who they were and stopped judging. I forgave them, and then, in my book, it became history.

You see, I put it in God's hands. My parents are good people whose lives are rooted and grounded in faith. My mom taught the catechism, and my dad is in the Knights of Columbus and feeds the poor. They raised us with love and taught us to forgive. They tried their very best; however, I was the firstborn and, some may say, the guinea pig.

I only saw my parents fight once—and that was a true lesson in forgiveness. One day, my brothers and I came home from school and saw our mother crying. As she never cried, we were surprised and asked what was wrong.

"Your daddy is mean," she said.

We saw that our dad was outside cutting the grass on the riding lawn mower. The next thing we knew, Mom brushed past us and walked down the street rolling her suitcase behind her. All the neighbors were watching.

All three of us ran screaming to Dad, "Mama is leaving us!" We chased her with my dad in the lead.

"Ginger, please come home!" he cried out. "I love you. I'm so sorry. Will you please forgive me … please, I love you. I'll never be mean to you again." When he caught up with Mom, he started kissing her.

My mom melted and looked at him. Smiling, she said, "Okay, I love you too. I forgive you."

Then we all went home and ordered pizza.

She dropped the discussion right then and there, and we all celebrated. My mom is the type of person who forgives and forgets easily. She acted like nothing ever happened, and we really learned a lesson in forgiveness that day.

Now that I reflect back on this story, it's funny because at that time, my mom had a brand new car in the driveway. If she really had wanted to leave, she would have gotten in her car and driven away. Instead, she rolled her suitcase down the road so my dad would have to apologize in front of the entire neighborhood. And she forgave him out in the open, too.

In my eighteen years of living at home, that was the only disagreement I knew about. It was a lesson I would use later in life to forgive my parents for the harshness I felt they showed me during my college years.

The thing is, no one is perfect. I'm not, so why did I expect my parents to be? My parents were good parents and are excellent grandparents today. So, in the end, I forgave them for what I perceived as lack of love. In the end, everyone came out ahead!

Get rid of all bitterness, rage and anger, brawling and slander, along with every form of malice. Be kind and compassionate to one another, forgiving each other, just as in Christ God forgave you. **(Ephesians 4:31–32 NIV)**

So, turn your life over to God and forgive everyone who has harmed you in any way. It's the only way to curb your judgment of others.

Do not judge, and you will not be judged. Do not condemn, and you will not be condemned. Forgive and you will be forgiven. **(Luke 6:37 NIV)**

When forgiveness seems impossible—do whatever it takes. Pray for strength to forgive others.

"And when you stand praying, if you hold anything against anyone, forgive him, so that your Father in Heaven may forgive you your sins." **(Mark 11:25 NIV)**

God forgave us, and always chooses to erase the board clean. He chooses to give us a new chance.

"I, even I, am He who blots out your transgressions, for My own sake, and remembers your sins no more." **(Isaiah 43:25 NIV)**

Jesus Christ shed his blood to forgive our sins. When we accept Jesus as our Savior, he forgives us.

In Him we have redemption through His blood, the forgiveness of sins, in accordance with the riches of God's grace that He lavished on us with all wisdom and understanding. **(Ephesians 1:7–8)**

I found out that when I forgave my parents, the layers started lifting. I didn't find an immediate peace, but I stopped distancing myself and avoiding my parents. We visited and communicated more and more.

Pray Every Day for Forgiveness

Forgiveness is a daily process. Every time a thought comes into my head that is not Christ-like, I try to catch myself and ask God for forgiveness. I do the same whenever I've judged someone. So, whenever hatred and bitterness, anger and blame come into my heart, I ask for forgiveness.

And when you stand praying, if you hold anything against anyone, forgive him, so that Your Father in Heaven may forgive you your sins. **(Mark 11:25)**

Whenever our hearts hold an unforgiving stance in relation to another person, we hinder our blessings. We block the pathway for receiving. **(Matthew 18:21–35)**

Then the master called the servant in, "You wicked servant," he said, "I canceled all that debt of yours because you begged me to. Shouldn't you have had mercy on your fellow servant just as I had on you?" In anger his master turned him over to the jailors to be tortured, until he should pay back all he owed.

"This is how My heavenly Father will treat each of you unless you forgive your brothers from your heart." **(Matthew 18:32–35 NIV)**

So, dear friend, let go of all grudges you are holding against anyone. I have a family member who always holds grudges. He says he doesn't, but it's apparent in his actions. Do you hold grudges, or do you forgive? Are you going to choose the elevator up to Heaven or down to hell? The choice is yours.

Let God take care of all the people who have wronged you. Let God take care of it … for vengeance is the Lord's.

I'm not saying you must have a personal, intimate

relationship with your enemies (for example, an abusive ex-husband or a hurtful relative). I only say that you must forgive them as God forgave you. Then your soul will be purified and a little more ready for the trip upward to Heaven.

When to Forgive

After Altercations
Bear with each other and forgive whatever grievances you may have against one another. Forgive as the Lord forgave you. **(Colossians 3:13 NIV)**

After Repentance
The sacrifices of God are a broken spirit; a broken and contrite heart, O God, you will not despise. **(Psalm 51:17 NIV)**

For a Closer Walk with God
Blessed are the merciful, for they will be shown mercy. **(Matthew 5:7 NIV)**

For Mercy
He who conceals his sins does not prosper, but whoever confesses and renounces them finds mercy. **(Proverbs 28:13 NIV)**

For Freedom and Dignity
I am the Lord, Your God, who brought you out of Egypt so that you would no longer be slaves to the Egyptians; I broke the bars of your yoke and enabled you to walk with heads held high. **(Leviticus 26:13 NIV)**

For Casting Out Revenge
Do not take revenge, my friends, but leave room for God's wrath, for it is written, "It is mine to avenge; I will repay," says the Lord. **(Romans 12:19 NIV)**

For Enemies

On the contrary; if your enemy is hungry, feed him; if he is thirsty, give him something to drink. In doing this, you will heap burning coals on his head. **(Romans 12:20 NIV)**

Prayer

*Dear Lord, Name above all names, I come to you today to ask you for endurance and encouragement to forgive others. I need strength so I can come to agreement with others. (**Romans 15:5–6**). Dear Lord, cleanse me of my hidden faults. Do not let my willful sins rule over me (**Psalm 19:12–14**). Help me to let go of illusions and false expectations of others. I want to speak and act with mercy and forgiveness (**James 2:12–13**). Lord, help me to be quick to hear, slow to speak and slow to anger (**James 1:19–20**). Lord, I release all anger, bitterness, resentment, ill-feelings, and hatred to you now. I forgive my family. I forgive my friends, and I forgive my enemies. Please help me, Lord, to put on your heartfelt compassion, kindness, humility, gentleness, and patience. Please help me to accept others and forgive others who have hurt me. Lord, please put love in my heart—the perfect bond of unity (**Colossians 3:12–16**). I do this and everything in the name of you, Lord Jesus, giving thanks to God the Father through you (**Colossians 3:17**), I pray. Amen.*

Chapter 8:
God's Gift of Patience

I thought I had it all figured out—regarding patience, that is. I was patient with my employees. I was patient with my family. I was patient with my perfectionist husband. I was even patient when housebreaking my two Jack Russells. No one could tell me anything about patience, as I thought I knew it all. If someone had challenged me, I would have said, "But I *am* patient. If you could only see what I deal with every day—my business, my employees, my vendors, and so forth—you wouldn't say that."

So, I really was very patient—at least until the day I lost it!

The nurses rolled my beautiful newborn baby boy into my hospital room. He was plump and wonderful at over eight pounds. My heart filled with joy. He had olive Italian skin like his dad and big, beautiful feet. I was in such awe over our first child, who was healthy, handsome, and asleep.

Then I saw his face and freaked out. It was bleeding, because he'd scratched it with his nails. "Oh my gosh," I said, "look at his face … my poor baby." I then asked the nurse why we wasn't wearing the mitts I'd brought. I'd even told the staff to make sure the baby wore the mitts at all times. I looked in the plastic crib, and the mitts were off to the side.

"How hard is it?" I asked the nurse, who'd stayed silent. "How hard is it to follow one simple request? Now my poor baby is bleeding to death!" The nurse still remained quiet.

She put the mitts on my son's hands and said, "I'll inform the nursery."

So, I'd bitten her head off over something that wasn't her fault. "I'm sorry for snapping at you, but I'm just upset," I said.

I was alone in my room, tired after seventeen hours of gruesome labor. The nurse was very patient with me, assuring me that his face wouldn't scar.

I fell asleep for an hour, and then my family started arriving and for the next several hours, I had forty people in my hospital room at all times.

Now, I consider myself a gracious, sociable person. But let me tell you, that day I was irritated and annoyed. The devil was trying to steal my joy. My nephews were chasing each other around the room. They knocked each other against the bed, making me want to scream and order them to stop running. Why wouldn't my brother control his children?

I'd allowed myself to lose my patience earlier with the nurse, and I've since learned that once you give the devil a little leeway, he will try to take over.

As I usually love company, I couldn't understand why I was so irritated. In fact, I would have been mad if they *weren't* there. The children running around would never have bothered me on a normal day. Even before I had my own baby, I loved children and had endless patience for them.

The devil was trying to tempt me to sin. Satan wanted conflict within my family because he is the author of confusion. He was furious that a miracle baby was born! If you've ever had a child, you will relate to this: when you have a child, you know and feel the power of God.

I could feel that power and joy—and Satan wanted to steal it. He wants to destroy any happiness that glorifies God. Satan's perfect plan was to tempt me into more sin. He'd already gotten me once that day and had me thinking all kinds of impure thoughts. However, I didn't give in to the desires of my flesh. I was able to avoid snapping at my friends or family who I'd invited to come visit me and my newborn son.

I didn't fully understand spiritual warfare at that time, but I shook my head to push the devil away. Looking back, I realize my fatigue provided the perfect entrance for the devil. He tried to get me when I was weak, which is how Satan works. He doesn't play fair. He will put negative and sinful thoughts into our minds to tempt us, and once the thoughts are planted, we may dwell on them. But our job is to choose obedience to God in all thoughts.

We demolish arguments and every pretension that sets itself up against the knowledge of God, and we take captive every thought to make it obedient to Christ. (**2 Corinthians 10:5 NIV**)

So, stay alert, take control of your mind, and don't let the devil take over your mind.

Be self-controlled and alert. Your enemy, the devil, prowls around like a roaring lion looking for someone to devour. (**I Peter 5:8 NIV**)

Satan uses tricks of the mind to get you to sin against God. If you notice, much violence and other crime, along with arguments among groups and families, happen when people are under the influence of drugs or alcohol, and the problems are often compounded by fatigue. Even murder is usually an act of rage that may grow from a seed of impatience and frustration, as left unchecked, those emotions may lead to anger and rage.

Get rid of the lust of the flesh and replace it with the fruits of the spirit. (**Galatians 5:16–22**)

Ask the Holy Spirit to help you rid yourself of lusts of the flesh, which are enumerated as: sexual immorality, impure thoughts, eagerness for lustful pleasure, idolatry, demonic activities, hostility, quarreling, jealousy, outbursts of anger, selfishness, ambition, division, self-centeredness, envy, drunkenness, desire to participate in wild parties, and other kinds of sin. These are worldly sins—the sins the devil wants you to commit. He wants you to produce bad fruit, which separates you from God.

Ask the Holy Spirit to control your life. Then you

will produce good fruit. You will then receive the fruits of the spirit: love, joy, peace, patience, kindness, goodness, faithfulness, gentleness, and self-control.

Have patience when things don't go your way. Don't get discouraged. And always remember: a delay does not mean a denial.

Trials and Suffering

Whatever trial you are going through, *stand steady and don't be afraid of suffering for the Lord. Bring others to Christ.* (**2 Timothy 4:5 TLB**) Of course, we will all go through trials and suffering—what would we learn about life if we didn't? It's these very hardships and adversities that strengthen our character.

I learned what patience was when I took my six-month-old, Isabella, to the doctor for a cough, and my entire world was turned upside down. The doctor told me that her platelets were so low that if she bumped her head, she could bleed internally and die in her sleep. What a shock! I thought the visit would be quick and I'd find out that her cough wasn't serious. I was terrified when the doctor said not to move her too much and to put the bumper pads back in the crib because she could have a platelet disorder, leukemia, or some other type of cancer.

Next, we had to have her blood tested three times a week. The numbers kept getting lower and lower, which caused me to panic every time I had to take her back to the doctor as I was terrified about what they might find. In addition, our Isabella had to endure the pain of having four large tubes of blood drawn from her little body.

Finally after a few months, the tests all came back

negative. But I nearly went crazy with worry and impatience.

However, I endured. I made it through extreme personal hardship, and God produced patience in me. I began to realize that delays are just part of life. I had to wait—I had no choice.

But these things won't happen right away. Slowly, steadily, surely the time approaches when the vision will be fulfilled. If it seems slow, wait patiently, for it will surely take place. It will not be delayed. **(Habakkuk 2:3)**

God had a plan, which I trusted, and that led me to surrender and accept His will. Because of my daughter's illness, I had to give up my job that I loved, but my baby needed me more. However, I kept my sanity, my family, and my friends, so I didn't reach the point of complete despair. Rather than giving up, I turned my heart toward gratitude and waited patiently for the Lord. When I decided to be patient, I didn't feel as if I were waiting. Feeling happy and peaceful in spite of what was going on, the days flew by. It turned into a blissful time.

Then one day I took my daughter to the doctor for her weekly blood count, and it was normal! Isabella was well, her platelets normal. No one knows what caused her to have ITP, Immune (Idiopathic) Thrombocytopenic Purpera. However, the doctor told me that it usually takes eight to twelve months to recover from ITP, and Isabella had recovered in just over two, so I knew it was God once again performing miracles in my life.

My Message to All of You

Like most people, I've had many discomforts in my life. Yet I found comfort in Christ, and I find joy in sharing my comfort with you. Whatever your problems are, or however much you are suffering, no problem is too big for our Savior to handle. Turn it over to the Lord. He will work it out.

Being patient and waiting for the Lord brings blessings. Don't give up and give in to the devil. Receive the blessings Jesus has in store for you.

Cast not away therefore your confidence which has great recompense of reward. For ye have heed of patience, that, after he has done the will of God, ye might receive the promise. **(Hebrews 10:35–36)**

Don't worry about your enemies and what they are up to. Prayer and patience produces miracles. Believe that and receive the truth. Then wait for your blessing!

Be still in the presence of the Lord and wait patiently for him to act. Don't worry about evil people who prosper or fret about their wicked schemes. **(Psalm 37:7)**

I promise, there *is* light at the end of the tunnel.

Prayer

*Most merciful Father, show me the way to Jesus when my enemies try to lead me astray. I wait patiently for you, my Lord. I will wait for you, brave and courageous, like your Word says (**Psalm 28:14**). Please help me to be patient in all things, small and large. Father, when I become overwhelmed by the burdens of this world, help me find the patience and strength to carry on. Father, transform all my desires of the flesh and produce in me the fruits of your spirit. The fruit I desire today is patience. Father,*

*I trust you with all my heart, mind, and soul to work your plan out in my life. I trust your timing, Lord. Help me to guard my mouth and keep myself from trouble caused by impatience (**Proverbs 21:23**). Lord, I want to be patient, waiting for healing, deliverance, love, and freedom. Lord, refashion me like a potter remolds his clay. This I ask for today.* [State your petition here.] *May my new gift of patience bring me closer to you in faith, hope, and love through Jesus Christ I pray. Amen.*

Here are some other teachings from the scriptures to guide you as you strengthen the quality of patience.

We do not want you to become lazy, but to imitate those who through faith and patience inherit what has been promised. **(Hebrews 6:12 NIV)**

But let patience have her perfect work, that ye may be perfect and endure, wanting nothing. **(James 1:4 KJV)**

Be patient, then brothers, until the Lord's coming. See how the farmer waits for the land to yield its valuable crop and how patient he is for the Autumn and Spring rains. You too, be patient and stand firm because the Lord's coming is near. **(James 5:7–8 NIV)**

Chapter 9:
Building a Relationship with Christ

In Chapter 1, I told you about the greatest love letters ever written, the love letters of the Bible. Let me compare them to genealogy, the way we learn about our lineage. It's wonderful to know where you come from, what your bloodline represents, and the way those who came before you looked, acted, and expressed themselves.

Likewise, the Word of God explains our true, divine origin. It tells us why Jesus Christ came: he came for me and he came for you. When feeling isolated or rejected, some might say:

"He didn't come for me. I'm not worthy. I can't have a personal relationship with him. I'm not good enough. I'm a failure. I'm full of sin."

Excuses! Excuses! Let go of all this garbage, as excuses

keep you from becoming holy. They separate you from the love of God. Let down the barriers of hatred, denial, and self-pity.

Think about this for a moment: God could have made us all alike, but He did not. He made us all unique and we are *all* special in the eyes of God. We have our set of fingerprints, evidence of our individual DNA. This shows us that God carefully took His time making each of us.

The uniqueness of everything the world has to offer is yours. All you have to do is love God and accept Christ. To accept Him means to believe in Him. To believe in Him is to love Him. When you really consider this, it's the easiest thing in the world.

God deeply wants us to be a part of Him, and He is touching each of us every moment. His touch says, "I am here to share my love with you."

Accept His love. Open your heart, mind, and soul and let Him love you. Let His love dwell in you. Let God become your everything and be obedient to the Word of God. When you do, you will find a deep, intimate, and abiding relationship by reading the Bible, praying, and trying to live a Christ-like life.

Reading the Bible

I don't know why this is, but it seems the hardest part of getting into the Word is picking up the Bible and opening it! But I've noticed that once we begin, once we learn how to approach and read the Bible, we gain infinite wisdom, knowledge, and understanding.

So, I advise you to read the Bible every day. Set a

time, perhaps only fifteen minutes or so. Then meditate on the message of each verse.

There are many editions and translations of the Bible on the market. My favorite is the *Application Study Bible, New Living Translation*. I have the personal-size edition and find it easy to read. I also like it because it has study notes on each verse at the bottom of the page. So, when I don't fully comprehend the meaning of the verse, I read the study notes, and it's as if a light bulb goes off in my mind and I receive true revelation.

A Bible doesn't do anyone any good by sitting on a shelf and collecting dust. Before you open your Bible, say a little prayer. Mine goes like this: "Dear Lord, speak to me through your word. Send the Holy Spirit to help me to have clarity, wisdom, and knowledge of your Word."

In my opinion, it's advantageous to start with the Gospel of John and then read the rest of the New Testament. After you've read the New Testament, start with Genesis and read your way through the Old Testament. Then, set aside some special time just for yourself to meditate and pray about the spiritual food you've received. When the Holy Spirit dwells inside of you, you will find truth.

But when he, the Spirit of truth comes, he will guide you into all truth. He will not speak on his own; he will speak only what he hears, and he will tell you what is yet to come. **(John 16:13 NIV)**

The love letters of the Bible will teach you, correct you, and train you in your spiritual journey.

For everything that was written in the past was written to teach us, so that through endurance and the encouragement of the Scriptures we might have hope. **(Romans 15:4 NIV)**

All Scripture is God-breathed and is useful for teaching, rebuking, correcting and training in righteousness. **(2 Timothy 3:16 NIV)**

Prayer and Meditation

Whatever amount of time you set aside, divide it into three parts. Spend one part reading the Word, another part in meditating on what you've read, and the last part in prayer. Here are some successful tips for prayer and meditation:

1. *Meditate on the Word of God.* Meditate on the meaning of the scriptures. The Word of God is your spiritual food, and helps you draw closer to your maker.

Jesus answered, "It is written: Man does not live on bread alone, but on every word that comes from the mouth of God." **(Matthew 4:4 NIV)**

2. *Praise God.* Thank the Lord for all the blessings you've received. Praise Him for all the blessings you've asked for. God gives life to everything **(Nehemiah 9:6).** Thank Him for your salvation.

3. *Sing Songs to the Lord.* He loves them! In fact, an entire book in the Bible, Psalms, is full of songs. Glorify God. Read **Psalms 151.** It is a good worship and praise song. When praises go up, blessings come down. So, praise Him today!

Praise the Lord. Give thanks to the Lord for He is good, His love endures forever. **(Psalms 106:1 NIV)**

Therefore, since we are receiving a Kingdom that cannot be shaken, let us be thankful, and so worship God acceptable with reverence and awe. **(Hebrews 12:28 NIV)**

4. *Pray for a Clean Spirit.* In order for your prayers to

be answered, you must go to the Lord humbly with the right motives and with a clean spirit.

Create in me a pure heart, O God, and renew a steadfast spirit within me. (**Psalms 51:10 NIV**)

5. *Pray for Yourself.* Ask the Lord for your petitions and converse with Him. Pour out your heart to the Lord, and always say the Lord's Prayer.

6. *Pray for Others.* Pray for others; pray for their souls to be rescued. Pray for family members, co-workers, enemies, friends, and lost loved ones. Pray for the softening of the heart of your enemies and for the poor, the sick, and the hungry.

7. *Surrender and Become Christ-like.* When you surrender yourself and your will to Christ, you then strive to be Christ-like. Of course, no one is perfect—not you, me, or your even your pastor. As Jesus offers forgiveness, when we repent of our sins, our slate is wiped clean. I've been known to repent five times a day, especially when I catch myself being impatient or prideful or wanting to gossip. So, I repent.

Some Christians abuse this power: they sin, repent, sin, repent, perhaps thinking of repentance as an "out." But we're called to walk the walk, not just talk the talk.

It's by the grace of God that we can receive salvation. Once we accept the Lord, we should have a reverent fear of the Lord. Growing spiritually is a must, and this process of becoming holy is called sanctification. It's the way we become Christ-like.

The angel of the Lord encamps around those who fear Him, and He delivers them. Taste and see that the Lord is good, blessed is the man who takes refuge in Him. Fear the

Lord, you His saints, for those who fear Him lack nothing. **(Psalms 34:7–9 NIV)**

To be Christ-like is to try to live as Christ lived and to follow his commandments.

We know that we have come to know Him if we obey His commands. The man who says, "I know Him," but does not do what He commands is a liar, and the truth is not in him. But if anyone obeys His word, God's love is truly made complete in Him. This is how we know we are in Him. Whoever claims to live in Him must walk as Jesus did. **(I John 2:3–6 IV)**

Let the Lord illuminate your heart and mind, to reveal to you what He has done for you at Calvary. If you walk in obedience and fear of the Lord, you will discover a newness of life. Believe by faith. Everyone feels different as they increase spiritually. Don't rely on your feelings—rely on faith.

8. *Live a Life of Faithfulness.* Make a determination, a pact with yourself that you will not allow anything to separate you from the love of Christ. Tell yourself, "I am strong. I am going to make it."

Become faithful to God in all circumstances. Faithfulness is not always what we want, but it is what we need most: it's what God wants us to do. I had an example of this last night when I'd gathered with my friends and family to watch a movie. However, my spirit told me I needed to write. Once I felt that conviction, nothing could change my mind, so I excused myself from the others and researched scriptures to write this very chapter.

Faithfulness is doing everything for the glory of God, even though sometimes it may not seem fair. Faithfulness starts with the little things. Some people try to change the world. They spend their entire life trying—and failing. No one can change the world. It is set upon a divine foundation.

I've spent time arguing and fighting when I knew I should have stayed silent. Sometimes we're vain and try to fight things that we have no business getting involved in. Jesus didn't argue every point, so why should I? Jesus was persecuted unjustly. Why was I any better? I should have been rejoicing that I was chosen to be persecuted. However, I didn't see it that way, and I was full of fight and fear, worry and despair, pride and self-centeredness.

One of the lessons I learned through a few bad, even horrific experiences is that humbleness and faithfulness go hand in hand. You cannot be faithful unless you are ready to be humble. Freedom doesn't come from arrogance. I should have just used what God gave me and let Him multiply. However, I tried to fix things myself. What happened? Despair, turmoil, hurt, and pain!

God doesn't need your help. He is in control and will supply your needs if you let Him. When hardship comes into your life, let God fix it. *What is meant to be is meant to be!* Pray and let God lead you in your actions. If you are faithful to God, He will be faithful to you.

Being faithful is getting up when you don't feel like it. It is setting a time to worship God and carrying through every time. Faithfulness is pressing through, although the journey is often difficult.

It is always easy to make excuses not to go to church, such as work, family, or fatigue—any excuse will do. Faithfulness is demonstrated by going the extra step to worship God regardless of your circumstances.

Satan is here for the long haul. He is waiting for you.

He wants your life and is trying to steal your soul. When excuses for not worshipping or going down a spiritual path come into your mind, rebuke the devil and say, "I'm saved. I am whole. Jesus is my Lord. Hallelujah!"

When you are faithful to Christ, you become branded. You stop looking all beat down and worn out. You will get your cup, and it will be overflowing. Yes, your cup will runneth over with blessings. Then you can take that cup and pour it all over the devil.

Be faithful … it pays!

9. *Redeem Your Soul.* When I'm trying to express an idea, I like to stress the meaning of words and caution that we need to watch our choice of them. For example, earlier in the chapter, I used the word "branded".

When you have a house and a car, you are branded, considered an owner. However, if you can't pay the mortgage or the car loan, you will lose them and they will have to be redeemed. *The American Heritage Dictionary* defines the word "redeemed" as: *to recover ownership by paying a particular sum.*

So, if you can't make the payments for one reason or another, your possessions will be taken away from you. Your blessings that branded you as a car owner and homeowner will be given to someone else, such as the bank that took over the notes, and you will need to redeem them to get them back.

We were all born sinners and branded as evil sinners. We were all born with original sin. However, Jesus came and redeemed us! Say these statements out loud;

Jesus redeemed me!
Jesus paid my debts!
I am redeemed!

It's all true: Jesus Christ paid our "sin debts" with his very life. By His grace, He died for our sins and offered us salvation. Jesus redeemed us from all original and mortal sin.

Salvation is not for sale; if you want it, you have to give Christ the reins of your life. In order to be redeemed, you must accept Christ in your life. You must give your life to the redeemer. To do that right now, say this prayer:

Prayer

Dear Heavenly Father, I confess with my mouth that the Lord Jesus is my Savior and Your Son. I believe in my heart that You have raised him from the dead. I repent of my sins right now [name your sins]. Behold, dear Lord, I stand at Your door and knock. Please send Your Holy Spirit to dwell within me. I believe I am now born again, saved and redeemed. Thank you, Lord, for redeeming me. In Jesus's name I pray. Amen.

Now you are redeemed! Now you are branded!

There is a song about being redeemed that I've always loved. Although I don't know who wrote the lyrics, I greatly admire the person who did, which is why I want to share them with you. They go like this:

I've been redeemed.
I've been redeemed by the blood of the lamb
I've been redeemed.
I've been redeemed by the blood of the Lamb.

111

Filled with the Holy Ghost I am.
All my sins are washed away.
I've been redeemed!
You can talk about me as much as you please, but I'll talk about you down on my knees.
All my sins are washed away, I've been redeemed.
The devil is mad and I am glad.
The devil is m—a—d and I am gl—ad.
The devil is mad and I am glad he lost a soul he thought he had.
All my sins are washed away. I've been redeemed!

Do you not know that your body is a temple of the Holy Spirit, who is in you, whom you have received from God? You are not your own; you were bought at a price. Therefore, honor God with your body. **(I Corinthians 6:19–20 NIV)**

You and I were born with a price. That price was the life of Jesus Christ. I take that very seriously, because Jesus gave his life up to save us, to redeem us. What have you done for him in return? Have you given your life to Christ?

You belong to God. He breathed life into you. You already belong to Him. You just have to find Him again.

Repeat these statements three times:

I belong to God!
I do not own myself!
God owns my soul!

Accept Him, and you will surely walk in the light.

This is the message we have heard from Him, and we declare: God is light—in Him there is no darkness at all. If we claim to have fellowship with Him, yet walk in the darkness, we lie, and do not live by the truth. But if we walk in the light, we have fellowship with one another, and the blood of Jesus, His Son, purifies us from all sin. **(I John 1:4-7 NIV)**

Some people think they are redeemed, and they will tell you they're Christians. However, they play games with God and have no idea what it's like to be redeemed. They may continue to lie, steal, cheat, curse, abuse others, have fits of rage, or become involved in sexual sins.

It's easy to use excuses for our actions. We may blame lack of self-confidence or peer pressure or a bad childhood. These are but a few of the lame excuses we use to justify our sinful behavior.

If there's something you don't like about yourself, if you know that you have sinned and want to find your way to redemption, just look for the root of the problem and claim it fixed in the name of Jesus. Realize that when you are redeemed, your "sin debt" has been canceled.

Remember: All you have to do for redemption is accept Christ. Once you accept and believe in him, every sin you have committed in the past is canceled. It was canceled by the blood of Jesus. Isn't that wonderful?

Once you are redeemed, you are *Christ-branded*. Those who are Christ-branded live lives of redeemed saints, and have royal blood flowing through their veins. Yes, that includes you! Once you are redeemed, you are royalty! Now stop all that sinful behavior and realize you are royalty and belong to Christ.

Ten Ways to Live a Redeemed Life

(1) **Tell the Truth.** Stop lying! It's always easy to tell a little white lie, but those "little" white lies always have

to be covered up with larger, more elaborate lies. Lies cause conflict and strife in relationships. They also cause unnecessary pain. The eighth commandment forbids all lies, false testimony, and judgments. *Each of you must put off falsehood and speak truthfully.* **(Ephesians 4:25 NIV)**

(2) **Control Your Anger.** Don't sin by letting anger gain control over you. Don't let the sun go down while you are still angry, because anger gives a mighty foothold to the devil. **(Ephesians 4:10–11 NIV)** Don't ever go to bed angry with your spouse or slam the phone down on a friend or relative. Resolve the problem, no matter how long it takes!

When you start to become angry with someone, confront the problem immediately. Holding anger in sometimes leads to a later explosion and loss of self-control. Volatile people often end up saying things they don't mean, thus destroying relationships. Remember, the devil lurks around, looking for a chance to enter your soul. That perfect chance is when you are tired, a little irritable, and you go to bed angry.

(3) **Be Honest and Productive in Your Work**. *If you are a thief, stop stealing. Begin using your hands for honest work and then give generously to others in need.* **(Ephesians 4:28)** The seventh commandment states, *Thou shalt not steal.* Redeemed Christians know not to steal. They also know that wasting time at work while "on the clock" is considered a form of stealing.

Don't waste what is not yours. Be productive in your work and honest in calculating your hours. Find honest and fulfilling work. And as a redeemed Christian, you should be able to use some of your earnings to help those less fortunate than you in their times of need.

(4) **Use Wholesome Speech.** *Don't use foul or abusive language. Let everything you say be good and helpful so that your words will be an encouragement to those who hear them.* **(Ephesians 4:29 NIV)**

My family and friends know not to use profane language around me. When an occasional curse word slips out of someone's mouth, I don't have to say anything in response. My facial expressions let them know that foul language appalls me, and they usually apologize. I find that my shocked reaction deters them from cursing more. It's a win-win situation because I'm also indirectly helping them by encouraging more Christ-like actions.

Erase all bitterness, anger, rage, jealousy, and bad attitudes in your life. Start living like a redeemed Christian, one who is free of all of those negative qualities. Show love! It's so much easier!

(5) **Be Kind, Tenderhearted, and Forgive One Another.** *Just as God, through Christ, has forgiven you.* **(Ephesians 4:32 NIV)** It should really go without saying, but please, always be kind to each other! It may not be easy, but try putting yourself in someone else's shoes. Picture yourself in that person's situation and treat him or her the way you would want to be treated. Rid yourself of vengeful feelings; forgive, forget, and love everyone with a tender heart.

(6) **Don't Play Games with God.** Let there be no sexual immorality, impurity, or greed among you. Such sins have no place among God's people. Obscene stories, foolish talk, and coarse jokes are not for you. Instead, let there be thankfulness to God. **(Ephesians 5:3–4)**

It amazes me how selfish people can be. Everything is about "me, me, me." They go after whatever brings instant gratification, including wild sexual sins, running with gangs, fighting, drugs, alcohol, and reckless driving. They may be motivated only by material gain while still expecting God to bless them. It doesn't and won't happen! God hates evil.

You have to choose God's way or your way. For example, it's not okay to have an affair if you are "out of town and no one will ever find out." God knows.

(7) **Let Your Actions Reflect Your Faith.** *For this light within you produces only what is good and right and true.* **(Ephesians 5:9 NIV)** Let the Holy Spirit guide you to set high moral standards for your life and for those you love. The Holy Spirit dwells inside of you now that you have accepted Christ. Bad decisions and choices cause the Holy Spirit to grieve. Fit compassion, kindness, humility, gentleness, patience, and forgiveness into your words and actions. Encourage others to find and accept our Lord and Savior Jesus Christ. Instead of giving extravagant gifts at Christmas or for birthdays, give a gift that will save a soul: a Bible. *Your word is a lamp to my feet and a light to my path.* **(Psalms 119: 105)** Lead others to Christ.

(8) **Rebuke Evil.** *Take no part in worthless deeds of evil and darkness, instead rebuke and expose them.* **(Ephesians 5:11 NIV)** Whenever you see evil, rebuke it immediately. If people you know are performing worthless deeds, tell them exactly what you think, then knowing that what they are doing is wrong, remove yourself from the situation. Expose to them their wrongdoings using the Word of God as your shield. They may get upset or mad, but believe me, they will think about what you have told them.

Do not merely listen to the Word, and so deceive yourselves. Do what it says. **(James 1:22 NIV)**

(9) **Live Wisely.** *So be careful how you live, not as fools but as those who are wise.* **(Ephesians 5:15)** Live as a Christian. Don't do anything in excess, from eating to smoking to drinking and so forth. These actions will ruin your life. Sing songs and hymns to Jesus. Keep divine standards, and always give thanks to the Lord for what He has given to you.

(10) **Live in Solidarity.** To live in solidarity is to live in unity with other Christians. Some Christians allow separations among them based on different beliefs in doctrine. To live in solidarity is to set examples that emphasize unity.

I knew a priest leading a mission in a South American country who taught a Bible study class. "Why was Jesus baptized?" he asked his students.

A woman raised her hand. "I know why," she said. "Jesus was baptized to give us an example. Jesus was a good leader, and he wanted to set an example for us."

Then an elderly man spoke. "I think Jesus was baptized out of humility."

Why do you think Jesus was baptized, even though he didn't have to be? Jesus was baptized to show his humanity and to fulfill the law. Jesus showed us an example of unity. All believers can experience unity through solidarity.

Solidarity is easy to apply to our everyday lives. It is about the oneness and unity of all believers.

All redeemed Christians are in unity with each other, through the Holy Spirit, through their faith, and through the belief in one God: the Father, the Son, and the Holy Spirit.

Shawn Kilgarlin

How to Apply Solidarity to Your Life

➤ *Learn* about other religions so you can better understand how others think.

➤ *Volunteer* to help organize a project for the poor in your community.

➤ *Visit* a nursing home and learn from the elderly through their life experiences.

➤ *Encourage* humble listening among your enemies.

➤ *Think* globally, *act* locally. Though it's always good to help the poor and homeless in other countries, what about the homeless in your hometown? Try to help them first. Show compassion and kindness in your local community. It still helps the global problem of homelessness.

➤ *Recycle*—when we recycle, we are doing something good for the environment. Recycling helps all Christians of all doctrines. If we save natural resources and eliminate waste, we will help all mankind. This will also bring all of us together as one.

Now that you are redeemed, you should dedicate and consecrate yourself to Christ, always being faithful to the Lord!

How to Consecrate and Dedicate Yourself to the Lord

➤ **Be Faithful in Prayer**. *Be joyful in hope, patient in affliction, faithful in prayer.* (**Romans 12:12 NIV**)

➤ **Be Devoted to Loving Others**. *Be devoted to one another in brotherly love.* (**Romans 12:10 NIV**)

➢ **Teach God's Word to Others.** *They devoted themselves to the apostles' teaching and to the fellowship, to the breaking of bread and to prayer.* **(Acts 2:42 NIV)**

➢ **Continually Consecrate Yourself.** *Therefore, I urge you, brothers, in view of God's mercy, to offer your bodies as living sacrifices, holy and pleasing to God—this is your spiritual act of worship.* **(Romans 12:1 NIV)**

➢ **Be Faithful in Prayer.** *Through Jesus, therefore, let us continually offer to God, a sacrifice of praise—the fruit of lips that confess His name.* **(Hebrews 13:15 NIV)**

Prayer

Lord, thank you for being pierced for my transgressions and crushed for my iniquities. Thank you, Jesus, for redeeming my life and my soul by the blood of the lamb. Thank you for snatching me from the power of death **(Psalms 49:15)**. *Thank you for delivering me from my enemies* **(Psalms 107:2)**. *Help me to live as your child, always walking in the light. I know that I will be saved on the day of redemption if I live in the light* **(Ephesians 4:30)**. *I dedicate and consecrate myself to you. My soul is thirsty of you, O Lord. I will drink from your Word. I reject Satan, the father of sin and the prince of darkness. I give my soul to you, O Lord. Please brand me as one of your children who will spend eternal life in your palace.*

Lord, fill me with hope. Grant me grace, O Lord, in this necessity …

Lead me into righteousness, Lord. I place my life securely in your hands, Lord. Bless me, protect me, heal me, and deliver me. In Jesus's name, I pray. Amen.

Dealing with Affliction and Adversity

All of us go through suffering in life. Sometimes, it is due to our wrong choices. Suffering, in and of itself, doesn't discriminate. Your suffering may come through no fault of your own. Maybe God is using you to be a vessel for Him. Maybe He is using you to be a testimony for Him.

And we know that in all things God works for the good of those who love him, who have been called according to his purpose. For those God knew he also predestined to be conformed to the likeness of His Son, that He might be the firstborn among many brothers. **(Romans 8:28–29 NIV)**

Your time of trial and adversity could very well be a test of your faith. God tested Abraham's faith and obedience. God told Abraham to take his only son, Isaac, and sacrifice him as a burnt offering. So, Abraham took Isaac, his son, tied him up, and was about to kill him when the Angel of the Lord stopped him. God was testing Abraham's faith, and Abraham proved to be faithful. Because Abraham was faithful, God blessed him.

"I swear by myself," declares the Lord, "that because you have done this and have not withheld your son, your only son, I will surely bless you and make your descendants as numerous as the stars in the sky and as the sand on the seashore. Your descendants will take possession of the cities

of their enemies, and through your offspring all nations on Earth will be blessed, because you have obeyed me." (**Genesis 22:16–18 NIV**)

When you are faithful through the hardest trials, God will reward you, and your reward will be beyond what you could ever dream. Consider it pure joy, my friends, whenever you face trials of many kinds, because you know that the testing of your faith develops perseverance.

Blessed is the man who perseveres under trial, because when he has stood the test, he will receive the crown of life that God has promised to those who love him. (**James 1:2–3, 12 NIV**)

When you are going through trials, surrender your soul to the Lord. He has sovereign power over every situation. It doesn't do any good to worry about "why" or "how" this could happen to you. Pity parties only make you feel pathetic. Go through your trial with a smile. It's easy for me to say this, because I've seen a miracle. I have also been humbled, justified (**Romans 4:5**), sanctified (**I Corinthians 6:11**), and accepted (**Ephesians 1:6**)!

Give Your Soul to God

(1) I got on my knees and cried out to the Lord.

For everyone who calls on the name of the Lord will be saved. (**Romans 10:13 NIV**)

I know He heard me, because "He hears the faintest cry." I asked the Lord to rescue me from my enemies.

(2) I repented of all my sins. I asked God to forgive me for all the sins I'd committed. This process spanned over fifteen months and continues today. Every time I think of any sin I have committed, I repent.

I even started to remember sins I'd committed when

I was a little girl. For example, I hid the car keys when I didn't want to leave a relative's house, and I remember eating all four bags of M&Ms in the freezer and blaming it on my brother. Then I started recalling lies I'd told my parents as a child. I repented of all of them.

Yet now I am happy, not because you were made sorry, but because your sorrow led you to repentance. For you became sorrowful as God intended and so were not harmed in any way by us. **(2 Corinthians 7:9 NIV)**

(3) I believed. *That if you confess with your mouth, Jesus is Lord, and believe in your heart that God raised him from the dead, you will be saved. For it is with your heart that you believe and are justified and it is with your mouth that you confess and are saved.* **(Romans 10:9–10)**

(4) I had faith. *But we are not of those who shrink back and are destroyed, but of those who believe and are saved.* **(Hebrews 10:39 NIV)**

Do not be surprised at the painful trial you are suffering, as though something strange were happening to you. But rejoice that you participate in the sufferings of Christ, so that you may be overjoyed when His glory is revealed. **(I Peter 4:12–13 NIV)**

I knew one thing: I knew God loved me. When I suffered indescribable pain, I prayed from eight to ten hours a day for a miracle. I pleaded with God for mercy, and I never lost hope, even when for a time it seemed the harder I prayed, the more bad news I got.

Yet I endured—and I never felt that the Lord had left my side. Sometimes when we suffer, we may think God has deserted us. When we feel this way, it is we who have turned away, not God. God loves us, and He is always there. He was with me throughout the severe trials in my life, and He's with you during your hardest times too.

I had to learn patience and hope, and God will teach you these virtues through your tribulations. Trust Him, and you will find glory.

Not only so, but we also rejoice in our sufferings, because we know that suffering produces perseverance; perseverance, character; and character, hope. And hope does not disappoint us, because God has poured out his love into our hearts by the Holy Spirit, whom he has given us. **(Romans 5:3–5 NIV)**

Handle Illness and Sorrow with God's Love

"Have I not commanded you? Be strong and courageous. Do not be terrified; do not be discouraged, for the Lord your God will be with you wherever you go." **(Joshua 1:9 NIV)**

When I truly, fully believed in His word, I started to sleep peacefully again. I knew I had favor with Him. Whenever you are saved, know that the Lord is by your side day and night.

"Never will I leave you; Never will I forsake you." **(Hebrews 13:5 NIV)**

Whenever you get scared, remember that God is by your side. Ask God to help you have courage. God sends angels to protect you always. Everywhere you go, angels surround and protect you. **(Psalms 91:11)**

You will not fear the terror of night, nor the arrow that flies by day, nor the pestilence that stalks in the darkness, nor the plague that destroys at midday. A thousand may fall at your side, ten thousand at your right hand, but it will not come near you. **(Psalms 91:5–7 NIV)**

Make God your refuge and no evil will overtake you. When find yourself afraid, trust in God.

When I am afraid, I will trust in you. **(Psalms 56:3 NIV)**

The Lord is my light and my salvation; whom shall I fear? The Lord is the strength of my life; of whom shall I be afraid? **(Psalms 21:1 NKJV)**

I often feel sorrow during times of distress and suffering. *What could I have done differently?* I wonder. I've felt discouraged, disappointed, and sorrowful during times of suffering. Have you? Have you let torment take over your mind? Maybe you blamed yourself for someone's death or you felt responsible for things outside of your control?

We all have faced adversity. I know individuals who were molested, abandoned, or neglected as children. I've known some people who've accidentally hurt or killed people in car accidents. Some of us have lost connections with our family over minor disputes. Some people have lived in torment for years.

God doesn't want us to live in self-inflicted torment.

During my traumatic experience, I berated myself and wasted time reflecting on every past mistake I'd ever made. I spent too much time in torment and sorrow.

Sometimes, God puts us through trials to bring us closer to Him. Godly grief that produces sorrow leads to repentance that leads to salvation. **(2 Corinthians 7:10–11)**

When we fall down, we often feel like failures. This could apply to failed relationships, high debt, loss of employment, and so forth. It's easy to feel like a failure in worldly matters. Dear friend, you must fail in order to later succeed. Just as everyone sins, everyone fails at something. **(I John 1:8)**

The key is to refocus on God and on learning from failure. To fail is not the problem; not getting up is the problem! When you fail, confess your sins **(I John 1:9)**, and as long as you confess them with your heart, God will forgive them. **(Matthew 18:21–22)**

You must have a comeback. That's the difference between failure and success, the difference between Heaven and hell. Get up and start over! Use your failures as strengthening tools!

Choose God's will, not your own.

Choose God!